THE REFERENCE SHELF    VOLUME 39  NUMBER 6

# TAXATION
# AND THE ECONOMY

EDITED BY

## GEORGE A. NIKOLAIEFF

THE H. W. WILSON COMPANY
NEW YORK            1968

# THE REFERENCE SHELF

The books in this series contain reprints of articles, excerpts from books, and addresses on current issues and social trends in the United States and other countries. There are six separately bound numbers in each volume, all of which are generally published in the same calendar year. One number is a collection of recent speeches; each of the others is devoted to a single subject and gives background information and discussion from various points of view, concluding with a comprehensive bibliography.

Subscribers to the current volume receive the books as issued. The subscription rate is $12 ($15 foreign) for a volume of six numbers. Single numbers are $3 each.

# PREFACE

A legal clerk, noticing United States Supreme Court Justice Oliver Wendell Holmes, Jr., filling out his tax form, asked the Justice if he didn't hate paying all that money in taxes. "No," replied the Justice, "I like to pay taxes; with them I buy civilization."

The Justice's view, though few would admit it while they were paying their taxes, is nevertheless commonly held. Most people realize that without taxes we would not have roads, police and fire protection, public schools, or any of the other amenities that make civilized society function. Nor is this view of recent origin. Ever since men first banded together there has been some type of system for the pooling of resources for the benefit of the whole community.

In very recent years, though, a startling new dimension has been added to the way in which taxes are used to buy civilization. When used in concert with other policies available to the Federal Government, taxes make an effective tool for pacing and directing a nation's economy. This is important because every nation wants to keep the level of economic activity at a steady, growing pace that provides jobs for all who need them.

The theory of how taxes are used to do this is deceptively simple. The key is control of aggregate demand—that is, total demand for goods and services. By encouraging this demand the Federal Government can speed economic activity. By restraining it, it can cool the economy. Taxes serve both as accelerator and brake in this operation. The more a person pays in taxes the less he has to spend on other goods and services, and vice versa. Multiplied by its effect on millions of people the adjustment of tax rates becomes a device that can slow a boom or curb a downturn with extraordinary effectiveness in an economy like ours.

Simple though this reasoning may seem, it was not a popular theory when first introduced, for it runs counter to classical economic doctrine which says no one should tamper with the economy at all. But classical thinking provides no solutions to reces-

3

sions or depressions and the suffering they can cause. Thus by the early 1960's this new theory—usually referred to as Keynesian economics after its formulator, Sir John Maynard Keynes—found acceptance in Federal circles. By 1962 it became part of the John F. Kennedy Administration's official policy. And in 1964 and 1965 the theory was translated into concrete action with the passage of two tax cuts. The tax cuts, economists now agree, extended good times into the longest period of uninterrupted prosperity the United States has ever known.

But then, and for some not unexpectedly, things began to go amiss. Not that prosperity has been seriously hurt. But by the spring of 1966 it became apparent that things were moving *too* quickly, that the boom was overheating, and that inflationary dangers were cropping up. And here the simplicity of the economic end of the theory began to run into difficulties.

Taxes, after all, have been a political entity far longer than they have been an economic tool. Congress controls the tax rates (other than those that are state and local). And for a public-opinion-conscious government raising taxes is far more difficult than lowering them. Then too, just when and how much action need be taken become matters of debate—debate that can often last far past the time action should have been taken. It is one matter to step on the accelerator when a tenth of the working force is unemployed. It is another matter to step on the brake when everything seems to be going all right.

Since the summer of 1966 the U.S. economy has been like a car that has gone into a slight skid. It is still going in the right direction, but the driver (in this case the President aided by his Council of Economic Advisers) is having to strive mightily to keep it on the road. Their efforts, most of which have consisted of moving various tax rates up or down as deemed necessary, have become the subject of widespread criticism and debate.

This book comes in the midst of this period of rapid-fire tax adjustments and the growing debate that the practice has triggered. Its purpose is to view the role of taxation as an economic tool. At the same time, because the two are so closely interwoven, the book also concerns itself with the fundamental economic assumptions that underlie our Government's actions in the economic sphere.

The first section takes a look at what this presently popular theory is, how it came to be accepted, how it was applied, and what its results were. The second section considers why the theory worked so well in 1964 and 1965. The third section focuses on taxation itself, how it began, how it evolved, and what it is today. The fourth deals exclusively with the year 1966, for in that period our faith in the workability of the theory was badly shaken as the economy went from controlled expansion to uncontrolled boom and then began nosing downward. The fifth section examines the shortcomings of taxation as a tool. The last section examines the whole spectrum of events and considers whether taxes will remain a tool of economic policy or whether the idea should be abandoned.

The editor wishes to thank the authors and publishers who have granted permission for the use of the selections presented in this volume.

GEORGE A. NIKOLAIEFF

November 1967

# CONTENTS

### III. Taxes Take the Limelight

### IV. The Reckoning

### V. The Human Element in Taxation

VI. OUTLOOK FOR THE FUTURE

# I. THE LONGEST BOOM IN HISTORY

## EDITOR'S INTRODUCTION

By the end of 1965 the United States was ecstatic over how strong its prosperity was and how long it had lasted. For five consecutive years the economy had been moving steadily upwards. Unemployment was down to 4.2 per cent of the workforce—the lowest level in a decade. It clearly looked as though the nation had mastered the kind of economic policy which—by mixing tax cuts with appropriate monetary policy—would maintain prosperity indefinitely.

The euphoria (for that it was) was all the sweeter because it represented the conscious application of an idea to a problem. British economist John Maynard Keynes had proposed that a free enterprise economy could and should be controlled and outlined how this could be done. Later economists added their own refinements. Together the basic theory and the added touches became known as the "New Economics," and then were translated into direct action—tax cuts whose sole purpose was to urge the economy onward. And It had worked.

The articles in this section deal with the immediate acts and ideas that came into play. The first selection, a *Time* magazine article, deals extensively with Lord Keynes, the early reaction to his theory, and the jubilation in the United States five years after his theory was put to work here. The next two selections deal with the specific theory and a fundamental assumption about public debt that allowed it to be put in practice. The next article, drawn, as was the second, from a review by the Harvard economist John Kenneth Galbraith, is a rare history of how these fundamental ideas were gradually accepted in this country, first at the academic level, then in Washington, and finally in practice.

The next selection, from the *Wall Street Journal,* describes the income tax cut and gives an idea of the broad goals the measure would hopefully achieve. The final selection presents President Johnson's statement recommending a reduction of excise taxes.

## "WE ARE ALL KEYNESIANS NOW" [1]

*The ideas of economists and political philosophers, both when they are right and when they are wrong, are more powerful than is commonly understood. Indeed the world is ruled by little else. Practical men, who believe themselves to be quite exempt from any intellectual influences, are usually the slaves of some defunct economist.—The General Theory of Employment, Interest and Money*

Concluding his most important book with those words in 1935, John Maynard Keynes was confident that he had laid down a philosophy that would move and change men's affairs. Today, some twenty years after his death, his theories are a prime influence on the world's free economies, especially on America's, the richest and most expansionist. In Washington the men who formulate the nation's economic policies have used Keynesian principles not only to avoid the violent cycles of prewar days but to produce a phenomenal economic growth and to achieve remarkably stable prices. In 1965 they skillfully applied Keynes's ideas—together with a number of their own invention—to lift the nation through the fifth, and best, consecutive year of the most sizable, prolonged and widely distributed prosperity in history.

By growing 5 per cent in real terms, the United States experienced a sharper expansion than any other major nation. Even the most optimistic forecasts for 1965 turned out to be too low. The gross national product leaped from $628 billion to $672 billion—$14 billion more than the President's economists had expected. Among the other new records: auto production rose 22 per cent, steel production 6 per cent, capital spending 16 per cent, personal income 7 per cent and corporate profits 21 per cent. Figuring that the United States had somehow discovered the secret of steady, stable, noninflationary growth, the leaders of many countries on both sides of the iron curtain openly tried to emulate its success.

Basically, Washington's economic managers scaled these heights by their adherence to Keynes's central theme: the modern capitalist economy does not automatically work at top efficiency,

[1] From article in *Time*. 86:64-67B. D. 31, '65. Courtesy *Time;* Copyright Time, Inc. 1965.

but can be raised to that level by the intervention and influence of the government. Keynes was the first to demonstrate convincingly that government has not only the ability but the responsibility to use its powers to increase production, incomes and jobs. Moreover, he argued that government can do this without violating freedom or restraining competition. It can, he said, achieve calculated prosperity by manipulating three main tools: tax policy, credit policy and budget policy. Their use would have the effect of strengthening private spending, investment and production.

## From Mischief to Orthodoxy

When Keynes first propagated his theories, many people considered them to be bizarre or slightly subversive, and Keynes himself to be little but a left-wing mischief maker. Now Keynes and his ideas, though they still make some people nervous, have been so widely accepted that they constitute both the new orthodoxy in the universities and the touchstone of economic management in Washington. They have led to a greater degree of government involvement in the nation's economy than ever before in time of general peace. Says Budget Director Charles L. Schultze: "We can't prevent every little wiggle in the economic cycle, but we now can prevent a major slide."

A slide, of course, is not what the United States Government's economic managers have been worrying about in 1965; they have been pursuing a strongly expansionist policy. They carried out the second stage of a two-stage income-tax cut, thus giving consumers $11.5 billion more to spend and corporations $3 billion more to invest. In addition, they put through a long-overdue reduction in excise taxes, slicing $1.5 billion this year and another $1.5 billion in the year beginning January 1 [1966]. In an application of the Keynesian argument that an economy is likely to grow best when the government pumps in more money than it takes out, they boosted total Federal spending to a record high of $121 billion and ran a deficit of more than $5 billion. Meanwhile, the Federal Reserve Board kept money easier and cheaper than it is in any other major nation, though proudly independent Chairman William

McChesney Martin at year's end piloted through an increase in interest rates—thus following the classic anti-inflationary prescription.

### Why They Work

By and large, Keynesian public policies are working well because the private sector of the economy is making them work. Government gave business the incentive to expand, but it was private businessmen who made the decisions as to whether, when and where to do it. Washington gave consumers a stimulus to spend, but millions of ordinary Americans made the decisions—so vital to the economy—as to how and how much to spend. For all that it has profited from the ideas of Lord Keynes, the U.S. economy is still the world's most private and most free-enterprising. Were he alive, Keynes would certainly like it to stay that way.

The recent successes of Keynes's theories have given a new stature and luster to the men who practice what Carlyle called "the dismal science." Economists have descended in force from their ivory towers and now sit confidently at the elbow of almost every important leader in Government and business, where they are increasingly called upon to forecast, plan and decide. In Washington the ideas of Keynes have been carried into the White House by such activist economists as Gardner Ackley, Arthur Okun, Otto Eckstein (all members of the President's Council of Economic Advisers), Walter Heller (its former chairman), MIT's Paul Samuelson, Yale's James Tobin and Seymour Harris of the University of California at San Diego.

First the U.S. economists embraced Keynesianism, then the public accepted its tenets. Now even businessmen, traditionally hostile to Government's role in the economy, have been won over—not only because Keynesianism works but because Lyndon Johnson knows how to make it palatable. They have begun to take for granted that the Government will intervene to head off recession or choke off inflation, no longer think that deficit spending is immoral. Nor, in perhaps the greatest change of all, do they believe that Government will ever fully pay off its debt, any more than General Motors or IBM find it advisable to pay off their long-term obligations; instead of demanding payment, creditors would rather continue collecting interest.

## To a New Stage

Though Keynes is the figure who looms largest in these recent changes, modern-day economists have naturally expanded and added to his theories, giving birth to a form of neo-Keynesianism. Because he was a creature of his times, Keynes was primarily interested in pulling a depression-ridden world up to some form of prosperity and stability; today's economists are more concerned about making an already prospering economy grow still further. As Keynes might have put it: Keynesianism + the theory of growth = The New Economics. Says Gardner Ackley, chairman of the Council of Economic Advisers: "The new economics is based on Keynes. The fiscal revolution stems from him." Adds the University of Chicago's Milton Friedman, the nation's leading conservative economist, who was presidential candidate Barry Goldwater's adviser on economics: "We are all Keynesians now." . . .

The U.S. economy . . . [at the end of 1965] is moving into a new stage. Production is scraping up against the top levels of the nation's capacity, and Federal spending and demand are soaring because of the war in Vietnam. The economists' problem is to draw a fine line between promoting growth and preventing a debilitating inflation. As they search for new ways to accomplish this balance, they will be guided in large part by the Keynes legacy.

That legacy was the product of a man whose personality and ideas still surprise both his critics and his friends. Far from being a socialist left-winger Keynes (pronounced *canes*) was a high-caste Establishment leader who disdained what he called "the boorish proletariat" and said: "For better or worse, I am a bourgeois economist." Keynes was suspicious of the power of unions, inveighed against the perils of inflation, praised the virtue of profits. "The engine which drives enterprise," he wrote, "is not thrift but profit." He condemned the Marxists as being "illogical and so dull" and saw himself as a doctor of capitalism, which he was convinced could lead mankind to universal plenty within a century. Communists, Marxists and the British Labour Party's radical fringe damned Keynes because he sought to strengthen a system that they wanted to overthrow.

## Truth and Consequences

Keynes was born the year Marx died (1883) and died in the first full year of capitalism's lengthy postwar boom (1946). The son of a noted Cambridge political economist, he whizzed through Eton and Cambridge, then entered the civil service. He got his lowest mark in economics. "The examiners," he later remarked, "presumably knew less than I did." He entered the India Office, soon after became a Cambridge don. Later, he was the British Treasury's representative to the Versailles Conference, and saw that it settled nothing but the inevitability of another disaster. He resigned in protest and wrote a book, *The Economic Consequences of the Peace,* that stirred an international sensation by clearly fore-telling the crisis to come.

He went back to teaching at Cambridge, but at the same time operated with skill and dash in business. The National Mutual Life Assurance Society named him its chairman, and whenever he gave his annual reports to stockholders, the London money market suspended trading to hear his forecasts for interest rates in the year ahead. He was also editor of the erudite British *Economic Journal,* chairman of the *New Statesman and Nation* and a director of the Bank of England.

Keynes began each day propped up in bed, poring for half an hour over reports of the world's gyrating currency and commodity markets; by speculating in them, he earned a fortune of more than $2 million. Money, he said, should be valued not as a possession but "as a means to the enjoyments and realities of life." He took pleasure in assembling the world's finest collection of Newton's manuscripts and in organizing London's Camargo Ballet and Cam-bridge's Arts Theater. Later, the government tapped him to head Britain's Arts Council, and in 1942 King George VI made him a lord.

Part dilettante and part Renaissance man, Keynes moved easily in Britain's eclectic world of arts and letters. Though he remarked that economists should be humble, like dentists, he enjoyed trouncing countesses at bridge and prime ministers at lunch-table debates. He became a leader of the Bloomsbury set of avant-garde writers and painters, including Virginia and Leonard Woolf, Lytton Strachey and E. M. Forster. At a party at the Sitwells, he met Lydia Lopokova, a ballerina of the Diaghilev Russian ballet. She was blond and buxom; he was frail and stoop-shouldered, with watery blue eyes. She chucked her career to marry him. His only regret in life, said Keynes shortly before his death of a heart attack, was that he had not drunk more champagne.

### The Whole Economy

The thrust of Keynes's personality, however strong, was vastly less important than the force of his ideas. Those ideas were so original and persuasive that Keynes now ranks with Adam Smith and Karl Marx as one of history's most significant economists. Today his theses are the basis of economic policies in Britain, Canada, Australia and part of continental Europe, as well as in the United States.

Economics is a young science, a mere two hundred years old. Addressing its problems in the second half of its second century, Keynes was more successful than his predecessors in seeing it whole. Great theorists before him had tried to take a wide view of economic forces, but they lacked the twentieth-century statistical tools to do the job, and they tended to concentrate on certain specialties. Adam Smith focused on the marketplace, Malthus on population, Ricardo on rent and land, Marx on labor and wages. Modern economists call those specializations "microeconomics"; Keynes was the precursor of what is now known as "macroeconomics"—from the Greek *makros*, for large or extended. He decided that the way to look at the economy was to measure all the myriad forces tugging and pulling at it—production, prices, profits, incomes, interest rates, government policies.

For most of his life, Keynes wrote, wrote, wrote. He was so prolific that a compendium of his books, tracts and essays fills twenty-two pages. In succession he wrote books about mathematical probability (1921), the gold standard and monetary reform (1923), and the causes of business cycles (1930); each of his works further developed his economic thinking. Then he bundled his major theories into his magnum opus, *The General Theory,* published in 1936. It is an uneven and ill-organized book, as difficult as Deuteronomy and open to almost as many interpretations. Yet for all its faults, it had more influence in a shorter time than any other book ever written on economics, including Smith's *The Wealth of Nations* and Marx's *Das Kapital.*

## Permanent Quasi Boom

Keynes perceived that the prime goal of any economy was to achieve "full employment." By that, he meant full employment of materials and machines as well as of men. Before Keynes, classical economists had presumed that the economy was naturally regulated by what Adam Smith had called the "invisible hand," which brought all forces into balance and used them fully. Smith argued, for example, that if wages rose too fast, employers would lay off so many workers that wages would fall until they reached the point at which employers would start rehiring. French economist Jean Baptiste Say embroidered that idea by theorizing that production always creates just enough income to consume whatever it produces, thus permitting any excesses of demand to correct themselves quickly.

Keynes showed that the hard facts of history contradicted these unrealistic assumptions. For centuries, he pointed out, the economic cycle had gyrated from giddy boom to violent bust; periods of inflated prosperity induced a speculative rise, which then disrupted commerce and led inexorably to impoverished deflation. The climax came during the depression of the 1930's. Wages plummeted and unemployment rocketed, but neither the laissez-faire classicists nor the sullen and angry Communists adequately diagnosed the disease or offered any reasonable remedies.

By applying both logic and historical example to economic cycles, Keynes showed that the automatic stabilizers that economists had long banked on could actually aggravate rather than prevent a depression. If employers responded to a fall-off in demand by slicing wages and dumping workers, said Keynes, that would only reduce incomes and demand, and plunge production still deeper. If bankers responded to a fall-off in savings by raising interest rates, that would not tempt penniless people to save more —but it would move hardpressed industrialists to borrow less for capital investment. Yet Keynes did not despair of capitalism as so many other economists did. Said he:

> The right remedy for the trade cycle is not to be found in abolishing booms and keeping us permanently in a semislump; but in abolishing slumps and thus keeping us permanently in a quasi boom.

## Management of Demand

The key to achieving that, Keynes perceived, is to maintain constantly a high level of what he called "aggregate demand." To him, that meant the total of all demand in the economy—demand for consumption and for investment, for both private and public purposes. His inescapable conclusion was that, if private demand should flag and falter, then it had to be revived and stimulated by the only force strong enough to lift consumption: the government.

The pre-Keynesian "classical" economists had thought of the government too. But almost all of them had contended that, in times of depression, the government should raise taxes and reduce spending in order to balance the budget. In the early 1930's, Keynes cried out that the only way to revive aggregate demand was for the government to cut taxes, reduce interest rates, spend heavily—and deficits be damned. Said Keynes:

> The state will have to exercise a guiding influence on the propensity to consume partly through its scheme of taxation, partly by fixing the rates of interest, and partly, perhaps, in other ways.

A few other economists of Keynes's time had called for more or less the same thing. Yet Keynes was the only one with enough influence and stature to get governments to sit up and pay attention. He was the right man at the right time, and his career and fame derived largely from the fact that when his theories appeared the world was racked by history's worst depression and governments were desperately searching for a way out.

Contrary to the Marxists and the socialists, Keynes opposed government ownership of industry and fought those centralists who would plan everything ("They wish to serve not God but the devil"). While he called for conscious and calculated state intervention, he argued just as passionately that the government had no right to tamper with individual freedoms to choose or change jobs, to buy or sell goods, or to earn respectable profits. He had tremendous faith that private men could change, improve and expand capitalism.

### Perhaps Immoral

Like any genius, Keynes had plenty of faults and shortcomings. Even his admirers admit that he could be maddeningly abstruse and confusing. MIT's Paul Samuelson, for example, thinks that Keynes downplayed the importance of monetary policy. His few outright critics feel that, while he knew how to buoy a depression-stricken industrial economy, he offered little in the way of practical information about how to keep a prosperous modern economy fat and secure. Keynesian theories are certainly unworkable in the underdeveloped nations, where the problem is not too little demand but insufficient supply, and where the object is not to stimulate consumption but to spur savings, form capital and raise production.

Such critics as former United States Budget Director Maurice Stans still worry that Keynes makes spenders seem virtuous and savers wicked, and thus subtly threatens the nation's moral fiber. Other doubters contend that earlier obscure economists originated some of the ideas that Keynes popularized, and that all he did was wrap them up in a general theory. But even his severest detractors bow to his brilliance, use the macroeconomic terms and framework that he devised, and concede that his main theories have largely worked out in practice. . . .

Congress adopted the Keynesian course in 1946, when it passed the Employment Act, establishing Government responsibility to achieve "maximum employment, production and purchasing power." The act also created the Council of Economic Advisers, which for the first time brought professional economic thinking into close and constant touch with the President. Surprisingly it was Dwight Eisenhower's not-notably-Keynesian economists who most effectively demonstrated the efficacy of Keynes's antirecession prescriptions; to fight the slumps of 1953-54 and 1957-58, they turned to prodigious spending and huge deficits.

### J.M.K. and L.B.J.

Still, Keynesianism made its biggest breakthrough under John Kennedy, who, as Arthur Schlesinger reports in *A Thousand Days*, "was unquestionably the first Keynesian President." Kennedy's economists, led by Chief Economic Adviser Walter Heller, presided over the birth of the New Economics as a practical policy and set out to add a new dimension to Keynesianism. They began to use Keynes's theories as a basis not only for correcting the 1960 recession, which prematurely arrived only two years after the 1957-58 recession, but also to spur an expanding economy to still faster growth. Kennedy was intrigued by the "growth gap" theory, first put across to him by Yale economist Arthur Okun (now a member of the Council of Economic Advisers), who argued that even though the United States was prosperous, it was producing $51 billion a year less than it really could. Under the prodding and guidance of Heller, Kennedy thereupon opened the door to activist, imaginative economics.

He particularly called for tax reductions—a step that Keynes had advocated as early as 1933. The Kennedy Administration stimulated capital investment by giving businessmen a 7 per cent tax kickback on their purchases of new equipment and by liberalizing depreciation allowances. Kennedy also campaigned for an over-all reduction in the oppressive income-tax rates in order to increase further both investment and personal consumption. That idea, he remarked, was "straight Keynes and Heller."

Lyndon Johnson came into the presidency worrying about the wisdom of large deficits and questioning the need for a tax cut, but he was convinced by the Keynesian economists around him, and hurried the measure through Congress. The quick success of the income-tax cuts prompted Congress to try a variant: the reduction this year [1965] of excise taxes on such goods as furs, jewelry and cars.

Nowadays, Johnson is not only practicing Keynesian economics, but is pursuing policies of pressure and persuasion that go far beyond anything Keynes ever dreamed of. In 1965 Johnson vigorously wielded the wage-price "guidelines" to hold wages and prices down, forced producers of aluminum, copper and wheat to retreat from price hikes by threatening to dump the Government's commodity stockpiles, and battled the nation's persistent balance-of-payments deficit with the so-called "voluntary" controls on spending and lending abroad. Some Keynesians believe that these policies violate Keynes's theories because they are basically microeconomic instead of macroeconomic—because they restrict prices, wages and capital movements in some parts of the economy but not others. Businessmen also complain about what they call "government by guideline" or "the managed economy," but not with total conviction. Business, after all, is booming, and besides, the Government is a big customer with unbounded retaliatory powers.

### Imitation Behind the Curtain

While the United States has been accepting the idea of more and more Government intervention within the bounds of private enterprise, many other nations are drifting away from strong central controls over their economies and opting for the freer American system. Britain's ruling Labour Party has become practically bourgeois, and this year scrapped almost all notions of nationalizing industry; West Germany's Socialists have long since done the same in an effort—so far unsuccessful—to wrest power from the free-enterprising Christian Democrats; and traditionally Socialist Norway in 1965 voted a conservative government into power for the first time in thirty years.

Piqued by the ideas popularized by Soviet economist Evsei Liberman, the command economies of Communist Europe are openly and eagerly adopting such capitalist tenets as cost accounting and the profit motive. East Germany, Czechoslovakia and other formerly Stalinist satrapies are cautiously granting more powers to local managers to boost or slash production, prices, investments and labor forces. State enterprises in Poland, Hungary and Rumania . . . [recently] closed deals to start joint companies in partnership with capitalist Western firms.

### Near the Goal

The United States right now is closer to Keynes's cherished goal of full employment of its resources than it has ever been in peacetime. Unemployment melted during 1965 from 4.8 per cent to an eight-year low of 4.2 per cent. Labor shortages, particularly among skilled workers, are beginning to pinch such industries as aerospace, construction and shipbuilding. Manufacturers are operating at a ten-year high of 91 per cent of capacity, and autos, aluminum and some other basic industries are scraping up against 100 per cent. Contrary to popular belief, industrialists do not like to run so high because it forces them to start up some of their older and less efficient machines, as many companies lately have been obliged to do.

The economy is beginning to show the strain of this rapid expansion. For the first time in five years, labor costs rose faster than productivity in 1965: 4.2 per cent versus 2.5 per cent. Consumer prices last year jumped 1.8 per cent, and wholesale prices rose 1.3 per cent, the first rise of any kind since 1959. This is already threatening the nation's remarkable record of price stability. The economy cannot continue its present growth rate at today's productivity level without serious upward pressure on prices.

### Growth Versus Stability

The economic policies of 1966 will be determined most of all by one factor: the war in Vietnam. Barring an unexpected truce, defense spending will soar so high—by at least an additional $7 billion—that it will impose a severe demand upon the nation's productive capacity and give body to the specter of inflation. Keynes feared inflation, and warned that "there is no subtler, no surer means of overturning the existing basis of a society than to debauch the currency." Once chided for undertipping a bootblack in Algiers, he replied: "I will not be party to debasing the currency."

The immediate problem that Vietnam and the threat of inflation pose to Washington's economic planners is whether they should aim for more growth or more stability. Labor Secretary Willard Wirtz argues that the Government should continue pushing and stimulating the economy, even at the risk of some inflation, in order to bring unemployment down to 3 per cent. Treasury Secretary Henry Fowler's aides argue just as firmly that the Government should tighten up a bit on spending and credit policy in order to check prices and get the nation's international payments into balance.

The man whose counsel will carry the most weight with Lyndon Johnson and who must make the delicate decisions in the next few weeks is the President's quiet, effective and Keynesian-minded chief economic strategist, Gardner Ackley. "We're learning to live with prosperity," says Ackley, "and frankly, we don't know as much about managing prosperity as getting there."

## The Sword's Other Side

Prosperity will bring the Government an extra $8.5 billion in tax revenues in the next fiscal year, and that means the United States can afford to boost its total Federal spending by $8.5 billion without causing significant inflationary pressure. If spending bulges much higher, the economists can fight inflation by brandishing the other sides of their Keynesian swords. Though Keynes spoke more about stimulus than restraint, he also stressed that his ideas could be turned around to bring an overworked economy back into balance. Says Walter Heller:

It should be made entirely clear that Keynes is a two-way street. In many ways we're entering a more fascinating era than the one I faced. Essentially the job is to maintain stability without resorting to obnoxious controls as we did in World War II and Korea. . . .

Economists in and out of Government are much more bullish than they were a year ago. The economy is not only running close to optimum speed, but has no serious excesses and few soft spots. Says Economic Adviser Okun: "It's hard to find a time when the economy has been closer to equilibrium than it is today." Orders are rising faster than production; wages are rising faster than prices; corporate profits are now rising faster than the stock market, even though the Dow-Jones average has jumped more than 400 points since mid-1962 and last week closed at an all-time high of 966. Businessmen plan in 1966 to increase capital spending 15 per cent; automakers and steelmakers expect to top this year's production records. Ackley and his colleagues anticipate that the gross national product will grow another 5 per cent in real terms during 1966, to $715 billion—or perhaps more.

## The Feeling Is Mutual

More meaningful than breaking records is the fact that the U.S. economy is changing for the better. In Lyndon Johnson's profit-minded Administration, Government planners have come to appreciate the importance of helping private business to invest in order to create jobs, income and demand. Johnson knows that he must have a vigorous economy to support his Great Society programs as well as the war in Vietnam and the United States' reach for the moon. To further that aim, he has more day-to-day contact with businessmen than any President since Hoover; he telephones hundreds of them regularly and invites scores to the Oval Room to hear their opinions. Under the atmospherics of the Johnson Administration, the United States has a Government whose economic policies are simultaneously devoted to Keynesianism, committed to growth, and decidedly probusiness.

Businessmen, for their part, have come to accept that the Government should actively use its Keynesian tools to promote growth and stability. They believe that whatever happens, the Government will somehow keep the economy strong and rising. With this new confidence, they no longer worry so much about the short-term wiggles and squiggles of the economic curve but instead budget their capital spending for the long-term and thus help to prolong the expansion.

If the nation has economic problems, they are the problems of high employment, high growth and high hopes. As the United States enters what shapes up as the sixth straight year of expansion, its economic strategists confess rather cheerily that they have just about reached the outer limits of economic knowledge. They have proved that they can prod, goad and inspire a rich and free nation to climb to nearly full employment and unprecedented prosperity. The job of maintaining expansion without inflation will require not only their present skills but new ones as well. Perhaps the United States needs another, more modern Keynes to grapple with the growing pains, a specialist in keeping economies at a healthy high. But even if he comes along, he will have to build on what he learned from John Maynard Keynes.

## THE GOSPEL ACCORDING TO LORD KEYNES [2]

It is a measure of how far the Keynesian revolution has proceeded that the central thesis of *The General Theory* now sounds rather commonplace. Until it appeared, economists, in the classical (or nonsocialist) tradition, had assumed that the economy, if left to itself, would find its equilibrium at full employment. Increases or decreases in wages and in interest rates would occur as necessary to bring about this pleasant result. If men were unemployed, their wages would fall in relation to prices. With lower wages and wider margins, it would be profitable to employ those from whose toil an adequate return could not previously have been made. It followed that steps to keep wages at artificially high levels, such as might result from the ill-considered efforts by unions, would cause unemployment. Such efforts were deemed to be the principal cause of unemployment.

Movements in interest rates played a complementary role by insuring that all income would ultimately be spent. Thus, were people to decide for some reason to increase their savings, the interest rates on the now more abundant supply of loanable funds would fall. This, in turn, would lead to increased investment. The added outlays for investment goods would offset the diminished outlays by the more frugal consumers. In this fashion, changes in consumer spending or in investment decisions were kept from causing any change in total spending that would lead to unemployment.

Keynes argued that neither wage movements nor changes in the rate of interest had, necessarily, any such agreeable effect. He focused attention on the total of purchasing power in the economy —what freshmen are now taught to call aggregate demand. Wage reductions might not increase employment; in conjunction with other changes, they might merely reduce this aggregate demand. And he held that interest was not the price that was paid to people to save but the price they got for exchanging holdings of cash, or

[2] From "Came the Revolution," a review by John Kenneth Galbraith of a reissue of John Maynard Keynes's book *The General Theory of Employment, Interest, and Money.* New York *Times Book Review.* p 1, 34+. My. 16, '65. © 1965 by The New York Times Company. Reprinted by permission. Dr. Galbraith is Paul M. Warburg Professor of Economics at Harvard University and author of *Economic Development* and other books.

its equivalent, their normal preference in assets, for less liquid forms of investment. And it was difficult to reduce interest beyond a certain level. Accordingly, if people sought to save more, this wouldn't necessarily mean lower interest rates and a resulting increase in investment. Instead, the total demand for goods might fall, along with employment and also investment, until savings were brought back into line with investment by the pressure of hardship which had reduced saving in favor of consumption. The economy would find its equilibrium not at full employment but with an unspecified amount of unemployment.

Out of this diagnosis came the remedy. It was to bring aggregate demand back up to the level where all willing workers were employed, and this could be accomplished by supplementing private expenditure with public expenditure. This should be the policy wherever intentions to save exceeded intentions to invest. Since public spending would not perform this offsetting role if there were compensating taxation (which is a form of saving), the public spending should be financed by borrowing—by incurring a deficit. So far as Keynes can be condensed into a few paragraphs, this is it. . . .

## THE NATURE OF THE NATIONAL DEBT [3]

By far the most common concern about the national debt comes from considering it as exactly the same kind of thing as a private debt which one individual owes to others. Every dollar of an individual's indebtedness must be subtracted from his assets in arriving at a measure of his net wealth. Indebtedness is impoverishment. It places the debtor in the hands of the creditor and threatens him with hardship and ruin. To avoid indebtedness as far as possible is undoubtedly an eminently well-established rule of private prudence.

The simple transferability of this rule to national debt is denied by nearly all economists. But nearly everybody who has ever suffered the oppressions of private indebtedness is tempted to ap-

[3] From "The Burden of the National Debt," by Abba P. Lerner, economist, formerly economic adviser to the Israeli government. Reprinted from *Income, Employment, and Public Policy: Essays in Honor of Alvin H. Hansen* by permission of W. W. Norton & Company, Inc. Copyright 1948 by W. W. Norton & Company, Inc. p 255-75.

ply the analogy directly, and the primary orthodoxy of the editorial writers, the dogma that sound government finance means balancing the budget, has no other basis.

One of the most effective ways of clearing up this most serious of all semantic confusions is to point out that private debt differs from national debt in being *external*. It is owed by one person to *others*. That is what makes it burdensome. Because it is *interpersonal* the proper analogy is not to national debt but to *international* debt. A nation owing money to other nations (or to the citizens of other nations) *is* impoverished or burdened in the same kind of way as a man who owes money to other men. But this does not hold for national debt which is owed by the nation to citizens of the *same* nation. There is then no external creditor. "We owe it to ourselves."

This refutation of the validity of the analogy from external to internal debt must not be interpreted as a denial that any significant problems can be raised by internal national debt. When economists are sufficiently irritated by the illegitimate analogy they are liable to say that the national debt does not matter at all. But this must be understood in the same sense as when a man who finds that rumor has converted a twisted ankle into a broken neck tells his friends that he is perfectly all right.

A variant of the false analogy is the declaration that national debt puts an unfair burden on our children, who are thereby made to pay for our extravagances. Very few economists need to be reminded that if our children or grandchildren repay some of the national debt these payments will be made to our children or grandchildren and to nobody else. Taking them altogether they will no more be impoverished by making the repayments than they will be enriched by receiving them.

Unfortunately the first few times people see this argument destroyed they feel tricked rather than convinced. But the resistance to conceding the painlessness of repaying national debt can be diminished by pointing out that it only corresponds to the relative uselessness of incurring it. An external loan enables an individual or a nation to get things from others without having to give anything in return, for the time being. The borrower is enabled to consume more than he is producing. And when he repays the external debt he has to consume less than he is producing. But this is not true for internal borrowing. However useful an internal loan may be for the health of the economy, it does *not* enable the nation to consume more than it produces. It should therefore not be so surprising that the repayment of internal debt does not necessitate a tightening of the belt. The internal borrowing did not permit the belt to be loosened in the first place.

Many who recognize that national debt is no subtraction from national wealth are nevertheless deeply concerned about the interest payments on the national debt. They call this the *interest burden* almost as if the interest payments constituted subtractions from the national income.

This involves exactly the same error. The interest payments are no more a subtraction from the national income than the national debt itself is a subtraction from the national wealth. This can be shown most clearly by pointing out how easy it is, by simply borrowing the money needed to make the interest payments, to convert the "interest burden" into some additional national debt. The interest need therefore never be more onerous than the additional principal of the debt into which it can painlessly be transformed.

Borrowing money to make the interest payments sounds much worse than simply getting into debt in the first place. Popular feeling on this score seems so strong that economists who are themselves quite free from the erroneous analogy have felt themselves constrained by the power of the prejudice to assume that the interest payments on national debt are never borrowed but raised by taxes.

The strict application of such a secondary orthodoxy would mean much more than these economists intend to concede to the popular prejudice. It would mean nothing less than the prohibition of all borrowing, and a meticulous adherence to the primary orthodoxy of balancing the budget at all times. For as soon as there is any national debt at all on which any interest has to be paid, *any* further government borrowing is indistinguishable from borrowing to pay the interest—unless we are taken in by bookkeeping fictions of financial earmarking which say that the money borrowed goes for other purposes so that the particular dollars used to pay the interest come from taxation. . . .

In attempts to discredit the argument that we owe the national debt to ourselves it is often pointed out that the "we" does not consist of the şame people as the "ourselves." The benefits from interest payments on the national debt do not accrue to every individual in exactly the same degree as the damage done to him by the additional taxes made necessary. That is why it is not possible to repudiate the whole national debt without hurting anybody.

While this is undoubtedly true, all it means is that some people will be better off and some people will be worse off. Such a redistribution of wealth is involved in every significant happening in our closely interrelated economy, in every invention or discovery or act of enterprise. If there is some good general reason for incurring debt, the redistribution can be ignored because we have no more reason for supposing that the new distribution is worse than the old one than for assuming the opposite. That the distribution will be *different* is no more an argument against national debt than it is an argument in favor of it.

## CAME THE REVOLUTION [4]

*I believe myself to be writing a book on economic theory which will largely revolutionize—not, I suppose, at once but in the course of the next ten years—the way the world thinks about economic problems.*—Letter from J. M. Keynes to George Bernard Shaw, New Year's Day, 1935.

The most influential book on economic and social policy so far in this century, *The General Theory of Employment, Interest, and Money,* by John Maynard Keynes, was published twenty-nine years ago last February [1936] in Britain and a few weeks later in the United States. A paperback edition is now available here . . . and quite a few people who take advantage of this bargain will be puzzled at the reason for the book's influence. Though

[4] From a review by John Kenneth Galbraith of a reissue of John Maynard Keynes's book *The General Theory of Employment, Interest, and Money.* New York *Times Book Review.* p 1, 34+. My. 16, '65. © 1965 by The New York Times Company. Reprinted by permission. Dr. Galbraith is Paul M. Warburg Professor of Economics at Harvard University and author of *Economic Development* and other books.

comfortably aware of their own intelligence, they will be unable to read it. They will wonder, accordingly, how it persuaded so many other people—not all of whom, certainly were more penetrating or diligent. This was only one of the remarkable things about this book and the revolution it precipitated.

By common, if not yet quite universal agreement, the Keynesian revolution was one of the great modern accomplishments in social design. It brought Marxism in the advanced countries to a total halt. It led to a level of economic performance that now inspires bitter-end conservatives to panegyrics of unexampled banality. Yet those responsible have had no honors and some opprobrium. For a long while, to be known as an active Keynesian was to invite the wrath of those who equate social advance with subversion. Those concerned developed a habit of reticence. As a further consequence, the history of the revolution is, perhaps, the worst told story of our era.

It is time that we knew better this part of our history and those who made it and this is a little of the story. Much of it turns on the almost unique unreadability of *The General Theory* and hence the need for people to translate and propagate its ideas to government officials, students and the public at large. As Messiahs go, Keynes was deeply dependent on his prophets.

*The General Theory* appeared in the sixth year of the Great Depression and the fifty-third of Keynes's life. At the time Keynes, like his great contemporary Churchill, was regarded as too clearheaded and candid to be trusted. Public officials are not always admiring of men who say what the right policy should be. Their frequent need, especially in matters of foreign policy, is for men who will find persuasive reasons for the wrong policy. Keynes had forseen grave difficulty from the reparations clauses of the Versailles Treaty and had voiced them in *The Economic Consequences of the Peace,* a brilliantly polemical volume, which may well have overstated his case and which certainly was unjust to Woodrow Wilson.

Later in the twenties, in another book, he was equally untactful toward those who invited massive unemployment in Britain in order to return sterling to the gold standard at its prewar parity with the dollar. The man immediately responsible for this effort, a highly orthodox voice in economic matters at the time, was the then Chancellor of the Exchequer, Winston Churchill, and that book was called *The Economic Consequences of Mr. Churchill.*

From 1920 to 1940 Keynes was sought out by students and intellectuals in Cambridge and London; was well known in London theater and artistic circles; directed an insurance company; made, and on occasion lost, quite a bit of money; and was an influential journalist. But he wasn't really trusted on public questions. The great public trade union which identifies trustworthiness with conformity kept him outside. Then came the Depression. There was much unemployment, much suffering. Even respectable men went broke. It was necessary, however unpleasant, to listen to the candid men who had something to say. This is the terrible punishment the gods reserve for fair weather statesmen. . . .

[For this writer's account of the core of Keynes' theory, see "The Gospel According to Lord Keynes," in this section, above.—Ed.]

Before the publication of *The General Theory,* Keynes had urged his ideas directly on President Roosevelt, most notably in a famous letter to the New York *Times* on December 31, 1933: "I lay overwhelming emphasis on the increase of national purchasing power resulting from government expenditure which is financed by loans." And he visited F.D.R. in the summer of 1934 to press his case, although the session was no great success; each, during the meeting, seems to have developed some doubts about the general good sense of the other.

In the meantime, two key Washington officials, Marriner Eccles, the exceptionally able Utah banker who was to become head of the Federal Reserve Board, and Lauchlin Currie, a former Harvard instructor who was director of research and later an economic aide to Roosevelt (and later still a prominent victim of McCarthyite persecution), had on their own account reached conclusions similar to those of Keynes as to the proper course of fiscal policy. When *The General Theory* arrived, they took it as confirmation of the course they had previously been urging. Currie, a highly qualified economist and teacher, was also a skilled and influential interpreter of the ideas in the Washington community. Not often have important new ideas on economics entered a government by way of its central bank. Nor should conservatives worry. There is not the slightest indication that it will ever happen again.

Paralleling the work of Keynes in the thirties and rivaling it in importance, though not in fame, was that of Simon Kuznets and a group of young economists and statisticians at the University of Pennsylvania, the National Bureau of Economic Research and the United States Department of Commerce. They developed the now familiar concepts of National Income and Gross National Product and their components and made estimates of their amount. Included among the components of National Income and Gross National Product was the saving, investment, aggregate of disposable income and the other magnitudes of which Keynes was talking. As a result, those who were translating his ideas into action knew not only what needed to be done but how much. And many who would never have been persuaded by the Keynesian abstractions were compelled to belief by the concrete figures from Kuznets and his inventive colleagues.

However, the trumpet—if the metaphor is permissible for this particular book—that was sounded in Cambridge, England, was heard most clearly in Cambridge, Massachusetts. Harvard was the principal avenue by which Keynes's ideas passed to the United States. Conservatives worry about universities being centers of disquieting innovation. Their worries are surely exaggerated—but it has occurred.

In the late thirties, Harvard had a large community of young economists, most of them held there by the shortage of jobs that Keynes sought to cure. They had the normal confidence of their years in their ability to remake the world and, unlike less fortunate generations, the opportunity. They also had occupational indication of the need. Massive unemployment persisted year after year. It was degrading to have to continue telling the young that this was merely a temporary departure from the full employment norm, and that one need only obtain the needed wage reductions.

Paul Samuelson of MIT, who, almost from the outset, was the acknowledged leader of the younger Keynesian community, has compared the excitement of the young economists, on the arrival of Keynes's book, to that of Keats on first looking into Chapman's Homer. Some will wonder if economists are capable of such refined emotion, but the effect was certainly great. Here was a remedy for the despair that could be seen just beyond the [Harvard] Yard. It did not overthrow the system but saved it. To the nonrevolutionary, it seemed too good to be true. To the occasional revolutionary, it was. The old economics was still taught by day. But in the evening, and almost every evening from 1936 on, almost everyone discussed Keynes.

This might, conceivably, have remained a rather academic discussion. As with the Bible and Marx, obscurity stimulated abstract debate. But in 1938, the practical instincts that economists sometimes suppress with success were catalyzed by the arrival at Harvard from Minnesota of Alvin H. Hansen. He was then about fifty, an effective teacher and a popular colleague. But most of all he was a man for whom economic ideas had no standing apart from their use.

The economists of established reputation had not taken to Keynes. Faced with the choice between changing one's mind and proving that there is no need to do so, almost everyone opts for the latter. So it was then. Hansen had an established reputation, and he did change his mind. Though he had been an effective critic of some central propositions in Keynes's *Treatise on Money,* an immediately preceding work, and was initially rather cool to *The General Theory,* he soon became strongly persuaded of its importance.

He proceeded to expound the ideas in books, articles and lectures and to apply them to the American scene. He persuaded his students and younger colleagues that they should not only understand the ideas but win understanding in others and then go on to get action. Without ever seeking to do so or being quite aware of the fact, he became the leader of a crusade. In the late thirties Hansen's seminar in the new Graduate School of Public Administration was regularly visited by the Washington policymakers. Often the students overflowed into the hall. One felt that it was the most important thing currently happening in the country and this could have been the case.

The officials took Hansen's ideas, and perhaps even more his sense of conviction, back to Washington. In time there was also a strong migration of his younger colleagues and students to the capital. Among numerous others were Richard Gilbert, now a principal architect of Pakistan's economic development, who was a confidant of Harry Hopkins; Richard Musgrave, now of Princeton, who applied Keynes's and Hansen's ideas to the tax system; Alan Sweezy, now of California Institute of Technology, who went to the Federal Reserve and the WPA; George Jaszi, who went to the Department of Commerce; Griffiths Johnson, who served at the Treasury, National Resources Planning Board and the White House; and Walter Salant, now of the Brookings Institution, who served in several Federal agencies. Keynes himself once wrote admiringly of this group of young Washington disciples.

The discussions that had begun in Cambridge continued through the war years in Washington. One of the leaders, a close friend of Hansen's but not otherwise connected with the Harvard group, was Gerhard Colm of the Bureau of the Budget. Colm, a German refugee who made the transition from a position of influence in Germany to one of influence in the United States in a matter of some five years, played a major role in reducing the Keynesian proposals to workable estimates of costs and quantities. Keynesian policies became central to what was called postwar planning and designs for preventing the reemergence of massive unemployment.

Meanwhile, others were concerning themselves with a wider audience. Seymour Harris, another of Hansen's colleagues and an early convert to Keynes, became the most prolific exponent of the ideas in the course of becoming one of the most prolific scholars of modern times. He published half a dozen books on Keynes and outlined the ideas in hundreds of letters, speeches, memoranda, congressional appearances and articles. Professor Samuelson, mentioned above, put the Keynesian ideas into what became (and remains) the most influential textbook on economics since the last great exposition of the classical system by Alfred Marshall. Lloyd

Metzler, now of the University of Chicago, applied the Keynesian system to international trade. Lloyd G. Reynolds, at a later stage, gathered a talented group of younger economists at Yale and made that university a major center of discussion of the new trends.

Nor was the Harvard influence confined to the United States. At almost the same time that *The General Theory* arrived in Cambridge, Massachusetts, a young Canadian graduate student named Robert Bryce arrived from Cambridge, England. He had been in Keynes's seminar and had, as a result, a special license to explain what Keynes meant in his more obscure passages. With two or three other Canadian graduate students, Bryce went on to Ottawa and to a succession of senior posts culminating in his present one as Deputy Minister of Finance. Canada was perhaps the first country to commit itself to a firmly Keynesian economic policy.

Meanwhile, with the help of the academic Keynesians, a few businessmen were becoming interested. Two New England industrialists, Henry S. Dennison of the Dennison Manufacturing Company in Framingham and Ralph Flanders of the Jones and Lamson Company of Springfield, Vermont (and later United States Senator from Vermont) hired members of the Harvard group to tutor them in the ideas. Before the war they had endorsed them in a book, in which Lincoln Filene of Boston and Morris E. Leeds of Philadelphia had joined, called *Toward Full Employment....* In the later war years, the Committee for Economic Development, led in these matters by Flanders and the late Beardsley Ruml, and again with the help of the academic Keynesians, began explaining the ideas to businessmen.

In Washington during the war years the National Planning Association had been a center for academic discussion of the Keynesian ideas. At the end of the war Hans Christian Sonne, the imaginative and liberal New York banker, began underwriting both NPA, and the Keynesian ideas. With the CED [Committee for Economic Development] in which Sonne was also influential, NPA became another important instrument for explaining the policy to the larger public. (In the autumn of 1949, in an exercise of unparalleled diplomacy, Sonne gathered a dozen economists of strongly varying views at Princeton and persuaded them to sign a specific endorsement of Keynesian fiscal policies. The agreement was later reported to the Congress in well-publicized hearings by Arthur Smithies of Harvard and Simeon Leland of Northwestern University.)

In 1946, ten years after the publication of *The General Theory,* the Employment Act of that year gave the Keynesian system the qualified but still quite explicit support of law. It recognized, as Keynes had urged, that unemployment and insufficient output would respond to positive policies. Not much was said about the specific policies but the responsibility of the Federal Government to act in some fashion was clearly affirmed. The Council of Economic Advisers became, in turn, a platform for expounding the Keynesian view of the economy and it was brought promptly into use. Leon Keyserling, as an original member and later chairman, was a tireless exponent of the ideas. And he saw at an early stage the importance of enlarging them to embrace not only the prevention of depression but the maintenance of an adequate rate of economic expansion. Thus in a decade had the revolution spread.

Those who nurture thoughts of conspiracy and clandestine plots will be saddened to know that this was a revolution without organization. All who participated felt a deep sense of personal responsibility for the ideas; there was a varying but deep urge to persuade. But no one ever responded to plans, orders, instructions, or any force apart from his own convictions. That perhaps was the most interesting single feature of the Keynesian revolution.

Something more was, however, suspected. And there was some effort at counter-revolution. Nobody could say that he preferred massive unemployment to Keynes. And even men of conservative mood, when they understood what was involved, opted for the policy—some asking only that it be called by some other name. The Committee for Economic Development, coached by Ruml on semantics, never advocated deficits. Rather it spoke well of a budget that was balanced only under conditions of high employment. Those who objected to Keynes were also invariably handicapped by the fact that they hadn't (and couldn't) read the book. It was like attacking the original Kama Sutra for obscenity without being able to read Sanskrit. Still, where social change is involved, there are men who can surmount any handicap.

Appropriately Harvard, not Washington, was the principal object of attention. In the fifties, a group of graduates of mature years banded together in an organization called the Veritas Foundation and produced a volume called *Keynes at Harvard*. It found that "Harvard was the launching pad for the Keynesian rocket in America." But then it damaged this not implausible proposition by identifying Keynesianism with socialism, Fabian socialism, Marxism, communism, fascism and also literary incest, meaning that one Keynesian always reviewed the works of another Keynesian. More encouragingly, the authors also reported that "Galbraith is being groomed as the new crown prince of Keynesism (sic)." Like so many others in similar situations, the authors sacrificed their chance for credibility by writing not for the public but for those who were paying the bill. The university was unperturbed, the larger public sadly indifferent. The book evidently continues to have some circulation on the more thoughtful fringes of the John Birch Society.

As a somewhat less trivial matter, another and more influential group of graduates pressed for an investigation of the Department of Economics, employing as their instrument the visiting committee that annually reviews the work of the department on behalf of the Governing Boards. The Keynesian revolution belongs to our history; so accordingly does this investigation.

It was conducted by Clarence Randall, then the exceptionally articulate head of the Inland Steel Company, with the support of Sinclair Weeks, a manufacturer, former senator and tetrarch of the right wing of the Republican Party in Massachusetts. In due course, the committee found that Keynes was, indeed, exerting a baneful influence on the Harvard economic mind and that the department was unbalanced in his favor. As always, there was the handicap that the investigators, with one or two possible exceptions, had not read the book and were otherwise uncertain as to what they attacked. The department, including the members most skeptical of Keynes's analysis—no one accepted all of it and some very little—unanimously rejected the committee's finding. So, as one of his last official acts before becoming High Commissioner to Germany, did President James Bryant Conant. There was much bad blood.

In ensuing years there was further discussion of the role of Keynes at Harvard and of related issues. But it became increasingly amicable, for the original investigators had been caught up in one of those fascinating and paradoxical developments with which the history of the Keynesian (and doubtless all other) revolutions is replete. Shortly after the committee reached its disturbing conclusion, the Eisenhower Administration came to power.

Mr. Randall became a presidential assistant and adviser. Mr. Weeks became Secretary of Commerce and almost immediately was preoccupied with the firing of the head of the Bureau of Standards over the question of the efficacy of Glauber's salts as a battery additive. Having staked his public reputation against the nation's scientists and engineers on the issue (as the late Bernard De Voto put it) that a battery could be improved by giving it a laxative, Mr. Weeks could hardly be expected to keep open another front against the economists. But much worse, both he and Mr. Randall were acquiring a heavy contingent liability for the policies of the Eisenhower Administration. And these, it soon developed, had almost as strong a Keynesian coloration as the department at Harvard.

President Eisenhower's first Chairman of the Council of Economic Advisers was Arthur F. Burns of Columbia University and the National Bureau of Economic Research. Mr. Burns had credentials as a critic of Keynes. In his introduction to the 1946 annual report of the National Bureau, called *Economic Research and the Keynesian Thinking of Our Times*, he had criticized a version of the Keynesian underemployment equilibrium and concluded a little heavily that "the imposing schemes for governmental action that are being bottomed on Keynes's equilibrium theory must be viewed with skepticism." Alvin Hansen had replied rather sharply.

But Burns was (and is) an able economist. If he regarded Keynes with skepticism, he viewed recessions (including ones for which he might be held responsible) with positive antipathy. In his 1955 Economic Report, he said, "Budget policies can help promote the objective of maximum production by wisely allocating resources *first between private and public uses; second, among various government programs.*" (Italics added.) Keynes, reading these words carefully, would have strongly applauded. And, indeed, a spokesman for the NAM [National Association of Manufacturers] told the Joint Economic Committee that they pointed "directly toward the planned and eventually the socialized economy."

After the departure of Burns, the Eisenhower Administration incurred a deficit of no less than $9.4 billions in the national income accounts in the course of overcoming the recession of 1958. This was by far the largest deficit ever incurred by an American Government in peacetime; it exceeded the *total* peacetime expenditure by F.D.R. in any year up to 1940. No Administration before or since has given the economy such a massive dose of Keynesian medicine. With a Republican Administration, guided by men like Mr. Randall and Mr. Weeks, following such policies, the academic Keynesians were no longer vulnerable. Keynes ceased to be a wholly tactful topic of conversation with such critics.

Presidents Kennedy and Johnson have continued what is now commonplace policy. Advised by Walter Heller, a remarkably skillful exponent of Keynes's ideas, they added the new device of the deliberate tax reduction to sustain aggregate demand. And they abandoned, at long last, the doubletalk by which advocates of Keynesian policies combined advocacy of measures to promote full employment and economic growth with promises of a promptly balanced budget. "We have recognized as self-defeating the effort to balance our budget too quickly in an economy operating well below its potential," President Johnson said in his 1965 report.

Now, as noted, Keynesian policies are the new orthodoxy. Economists are everywhere to be seen enjoying their new and pleasantly uncontroversial role. Like their predecessors who averted their eyes from unemployment, many are now able to ignore— often with some slight note of scholarly righteousness—the new problem, which is an atrocious allocation of resources between private wants and public needs, especially those of our cities. (In a sense, the Keynesian success has brought back an older problem of economics, that of resource allocation, in a new form.) And there is the dangerously high dependence on military spending. But these are other matters.

We have yet to pay proper respect to those who pioneered the Keynesian revolution. Everyone now takes pride in the resulting performance of the economy. We should take a little pride in the men who brought it about. It is hardly fitting that they should have been celebrated only by the reactionaries. The debt to the courage and intelligence of Alvin Hansen is especially great. Next only to Keynes, his is the credit for saving what even conservatives still call capitalism.

## THE FIRST TAX CUT, 1964 [5]

President Johnson signed the $11.5 billion tax-cut bill yesterday [February 26, 1964] thus firing the Administration's biggest economic gun.

The Government will be waiting anxiously for the widely predicted boom.

The bill took the last step in its thirteen-month trek around Capitol Hill shortly after noon, when the Senate endorsed the compromise worked out last week with House conferees. The Senate vote was 74 to 19—with 53 Democrats and 21 Republicans voting in favor and 10 Democrats and 9 Republicans against.

At the White House the President followed last evening's bill-signing ceremony with a televised address emphasizing the Administration's fond hopes for the tax cut, "the single most important step that we have taken to strengthen our economy since World War II."

But he also warned that this "bold approach"—economic stimulus achieved by cutting taxes rather than raising Federal outlays —will work best only if the money that would have gone for taxes is poured into the commercial stream: "Then the Federal Government will not have to do for the economy what the economy should do for itself."

The first effect of the tax cut will be seen in paychecks dated Thursday, March 5, and thereafter, when the rate at which income taxes are withheld drops to 14 per cent from the present 18 per cent.

[5] From "Waiting for the Boom," by Richard F. Janssen, staff reporter. *Wall Street Journal.* p 3, 12. F. 27, '64. Reprinted by permission.

The bill, embraced by groups that are usually poles apart, such as the AFL-CIO and the U.S. Chamber of Commerce, is envisioned as providing:

More money for consumers
Higher profits for business
Added jobs
Reinforcements for the gold supply
Broad levelers for the business cycle
New restraints on Government spending
And extra impetus for the antipoverty drive

But it is conceded that the bill's blessings aren't unmixed. White House authorities acknowledge that rising prosperity could tempt businessmen to raise prices and whet labor's appetite for wage increases.

### Inflation Threat

If the President's appeals for price and wage restraints don't prove effective, dormant inflationary fires could be rekindled. The Federal Reserve Board has made clear it would act to dampen them, possibly by prodding a rise in interest rates. This could modify any general expansion, something the President has urged the Board to carefully avoid.

The opinions among both supporters and critics of the tax bill vary widely.

Some liberals in Congress fear the Government will slice its revenues so much that it will lose the flexibility to cope with any future recession by cutting taxes again or by sharply stepping up spending.

Some conservatives in Congress worry that a recession threat is much more immediate, and that overstimulation this year to a pace that can't be maintained will leave the economy out of breath next year.

Other people say the bill doesn't do enough for the poor. Still others contend it does too much for the poor and not enough for the rich, who, they say, should be encouraged to accumulate money to invest in future economic development.

To know that praise and blame alike are coming from both ends of the political pendulum encourages the Administration men's belief that they are on the right track. Moreover, they strongly defend the research into economic history, principally European, that helped them prepare their forecasts of the tax cut's benefits.

### The "Testing Time"

When pressed, however, they concede that all their predictions are based on theories. As Treasury Secretary Dillon told Congress last month, it will be sometime in 1966 before it is really known if "these theories will work as well here as they have in other countries." The fiscal year starting July 1, 1966, and not the next few months, will be the real "testing time," he said.

Top officials dismiss the contention of some critics that the biggest effect has already been felt as individuals and businesses increased fall and winter spending in anticipation of the lower taxes this year. Washington authorities don't doubt that optimism about the tax cut has helped sustain the business pace in recent months, but they reject the suggestion that all the extra money was spent before it was absolutely assured.

In the Treasury's view, the lower withholding rates won't strongly stimulate consumer spending until the coming fall or winter. It feels a family will need to accumulate the extra dollars before it can spend them for a television set or a vacation. It also believes a corporation's building plans can't immediately be translated into actual outlays. As private spending gains momentum, it says Federal spending should start tapering off, according to the tightened budget President Johnson has proposed for the fiscal year starting July 1. The coinciding of these two predicted opposite forces has been described by Mr. Dillon as a "perfect mix," just right to absorb any inflationary impact but not enough to stunt expected growth.

Some Federal Reserve Board officials are more optimistic about a quick stimulus from the tax cut and more pessimistic about inflationary dangers. They expect consumers to quickly spend at least their extra disposable income, if not more, and they say that by midsummer this growing demand will be pushing up prices.

About the same time, these experts figure, wages will be rising; they aren't sanguine about the President's pleas for restraint, or about the Government's "guideposts" for keeping price and wage increases in line with the national productivity increase, which the Administration calculates at 3.2 per cent a year. In recent days, AFL-CIO President George Meany served notice that the guideposts won't stand between his union and whatever pay raises it can obtain.

Federal Reserve officials, who can influence interest costs by a variety of means other than the discount rate charged by their district banks on loans to member banks, hope the tax cut won't compel any overt action on their part. They expect rather that if demand for credit expands as a result of business optimism, borrowing costs could rise by themselves. In that case they might achieve their aims by doing nothing to interfere with any free-market rise in interest rates and its expected dampening of any inflationary flames....

### Aid for Gold Supply

Looking far ahead, Government experts see the lowered manufacturing costs that result from the increased efficiency helping save the United States gold supply and keeping the whole free world economy running smoothly. They argue lower-cost production will allow U.S. companies to sell more goods abroad and to compete better with imports at home, though there is no doubt consumers will spend some tax savings on foreign cars and other imports.

The United States already sells more abroad than it imports, but this trade surplus is more than offset by private U.S. capital investments abroad and outflows the Government figures it can't discontinue without impairing security, notably foreign aid and defense spending. More efficient and profitable industry at home should also help keep private investment dollars here, thus going a long way toward ending the recently shrinking balance-of-payments deficit, it is figured. The surplus dollars foreign governments have been acquiring can be used to buy United States gold; this stock, a mainstay of world currency stability, has been dwindling.

Administration economists hope the tax cut not only will give a lift to today's economy but will make future recessions less frequent and less severe. Mr. Johnson doesn't promise that it could "legislate the business cycle out of existence," but contends it can help "prevent some recessions and nip others in the bud." A more immediate task of the tax cut will be to stretch out the present expansion into the longest peacetime one, topping the long pull out of the depression of the 1930's.

Often overlooked in discussing the tax program, Administration men say, is that it represents a historic turning point, an end to increasing reliance on Federal policy to stimulate the economy. As Treasury Secretary Dillon says, it reflects "a deliberate decision to rely upon the private sector of the economy to provide the motive force for the more rapid economic progress that our situation demands."

Some critics, of course, view the move as a reckless political move to influence voters by cutting taxes when they aren't even high enough to cover Federal spending. . . . As for President Johnson's "war on poverty," . . . Government experts concede the tax cut by itself won't win the war. But only in "a more buoyant economic environment," says Secretary Dillon, can such specific weapons as job retraining and bias-free hiring be fully effective.

"The greatest single step that can be taken to speed the creation of new job opportunities," Mr. Dillon concludes, involves "lifting from the private economy the shackles of wartime tax rates."

## THE SECOND CUT, 1965 [6]

Fourteen months ago, I signed the Revenue Act of 1964, which reduced the income taxes of the American people by $14 billion. [The amount is the total tax saving in fourteen months—Ed.]

This action had a profound impact on the American economy: Consumer buying rose by $28 billion.

Business investment in plant and equipment rose $6.5 billion.

Almost two million new jobs were created, and unemployment fell to the lowest level in seven years.

[6] President Lyndon B. Johnson's message to Congress, May 17, 1965. Text from New York *Times*. p 26. My. 18, '65.

Meanwhile, the stability of our prices—unmatched in the world today—held firm and our foreign trade surplus set new records.

I am proud of the success of the 1964 tax cut. It proves that taxes do much more than raise revenue to finance the Government—they also affect the health and strength of the nation's economy.

Unwise tax policy can:

Unduly restrict private purchasing power
Hold back economic growth
Stifle incentive
Distort decisions by consumers and producers
Enlarge rather than shrink budget deficits

On the other hand, wise tax policy can:

Raise the purchasing power of private citizens
Expand production and create jobs
Stimulate initiative and improve efficiency

Reduce budget deficits by expanding the tax base and increase tax revenues

We used tax policy last year to achieve those goals.

As a result, this month we passed a milestone in economic history; more than fifty months of unbroken peacetime expansion.

But we cannot stand still. We must continually adjust our tax system to assure that it makes a maximum contribution to our economic growth.

For that reason I am recommending reductions in excise taxes as well as increases in user charges.

### Excise Taxes

I recommend an excise tax reduction of $3.5 billion in two equal stages effective July 1, 1965, and January 1, 1966.

I also recommend further reductions on January 1 of each year from 1967 through 1969 totaling $464 million.

Many of our existing excises were born of depression and war. Many were designed to restrain civilian demands in wartime and thereby free resources for military use. They need to be reexamined to assure that they do not hold back an expanding peacetime economy.

The proposed program of excise tax cuts and revisions will spur growth and move us closer to full employment by removing an unnecessary drag on consumer and business purchasing power. It will also:

Lower prices to consumers

Lessen the burden of regressive taxes on low-income families

Raise business profits by expanding sales and cutting costs of tax compliance

Cut the Government's costs of tax collection and enforcement

End an unfair burden on many businesses and workers who produce the commodities singled out for excise taxation

Free consumers from the distorting effects of these taxes on their market choices

### The Program of Excise Tax Reduction

In the budget for fiscal year 1966 I proposed an excise tax reduction of $1.75 billion effective July 1, 1965, and an increase in user charges of $300 million.

Our improving fiscal position, together with our developing economic situation, now makes it possible and desirable to double the recommended excise tax cut.

Responding strongly to an expanding economy, revenues for both fiscal years 1965 and 1966 are now estimated substantially higher than our conservative January estimates.

For fiscal 1965, we now expect revenues to be $1.4 billion above the January figure of $91.2 billion.

For fiscal 1966, we now anticipate—given the tax program as proposed in January—that revenues would be about $1.6 billion above the January estimate of $94.4 billion.

We can make the recommended tax cuts and still realize total revenues well above—and a deficit well below—our earlier estimates for fiscal 1966.

### Buying Power Cited

Because the progress of the United States economy in 1965 is living up to our expectations, the January proposal for a $1.75 billion reduction this July continues to be appropriate.

But as we look ahead to 1966, we must be alert to the possibility that our taxes will take too much buying power out of the private economy. To foster continued strong expansion of the economy in 1966, I am recommending an additional $1.75 billion reduction of excise taxes, effective January 1, 1966.

The revenue impact on the fiscal 1966 budget of the additional reduction—which will affect only the last half of the fiscal year—will be about $600 million. This will leave a substantial portion of the anticipated increase in revenues above the January budget estimate to reduce the estimated budget deficit.

The reductions I am recommending will accomplish, prudently and responsibly, a major reform of the excise tax structure. We will:

Eliminate most of our present excise taxes on July 1, 1965, and even more on January 1, 1966;

Eliminate the tax on telephone service, in several steps, by January 1, 1969;

Gradually reduce the automobile excise tax from 10 per cent now to 5 per cent by January 1, 1967;

Leave only, in addition, the excises on alcoholic beverages, tobacco, gasoline, tires, trucks, air transportation (and a few other user-charge and special excises) which should remain a part of our tax system.

## Excise Tax Reduction, Defense, and the Nation's Economy

In proposing these reductions, I am fully aware of our present and prospective commitments for the defense of the free world. It is impossible to predict precisely what expenditures these may involve in the future. There is, however, no present indication that expenditures will increase to an extent that would make these excise tax reductions inadvisable.

Indeed, our international responsibilities require that we redouble our efforts to assure the continued healthy growth of our economy. Barring some sudden change in the present world situation, I am sure that these excise tax reductions will be a sound and profitable investment in that growth.

[President Johnson's recommendation became a bill, was passed by both houses, and was sent back for the President's signature on

June 17, 1965. The bill contained substantially all the requested cuts that the President had proposed and that were to have taken effect over a period of years. However, as the Federal Government's need for revenues increased, the effective dates for some of these cuts were postponed.

For example, excise taxes on both automobile sales and telephone service—the two largest revenue producers to be reduced in the 1965 cut—were reinstated either in full or in part very quickly. The manufacturer's excise tax on automobiles, which in fiscal 1966 totaled $2,148,840, was initially cut from 10 per cent to 7 per cent on July 1, 1965, and then again cut to 6 per cent on January 1, 1966. By January 1, 1969 this levy was slated to drop to only 1 per cent. However, on March 15, 1966, two and one half months after going from 7 per cent to 6 per cent, the tax was boosted back to 7 per cent, where it has remained since. Similarly on telephone service the tax was first reduced from 10 per cent to 3 per cent on January 1, 1966. Then on April 1, 1966, it was boosted back to 10 per cent. Telephone service excise taxes in fiscal 1966 gathered nearly a billion dollars in revenue.—Ed.]

## II. WHY DID IT WORK?

### EDITOR'S INTRODUCTION

Why did the "new economics" work? There was, of course, the theory, there were the refinements, and there ultimately was the will to put them to use. But these are only tools and no amount of good intentions could make them work unless the need to use them is pressing enough and the proper conditions, both legal and structural, have first been met.

In this section the focus is on the fundamental assumptions and conditions that created the appropriate groundwork for the application of the new economics. The first article, by economist Milton Gilbert, delves into the reasoning that led to the Employment Act of 1946. This bill is a milestone in American history, for it placed the legal responsibility for creating a prosperous economy in the hands of the Federal Government. It also created some of the machinery for managing the total economy—for example, the thorough collection of data on which decisions would be made and the President's Council of Economic Advisers, whose job is to watch over the health of the economy.

The W.W. Rostow piece that follows charts the evolution of our economy into one characterized by mass consumption. This condition is a fact of paramount importance in determining economic policies. In an undeveloped country, for example, prosperity comes when productive facilities are at last able to create enough to satisfy the needs of the population. But in a developed country productive facilities (almost by definition) are already plentiful. Thus in a country like the United States consumption must be high enough to keep productive machinery working. This means that economists must concern themselves with keeping mass demand high enough to keep the nation prosperous.

The third article deals with still another fundamental issue— just how fast should a nation grow? We have become so accustomed to the notion that the economy must grow that we often forget why it should—and there are very cogent reasons for it, as British economist Barbara Ward deftly points out in her article.

The next selection is a 1959 *Time* magazine article that questions whether the U.S. economy is growing fast enough. It is worth noting that while the topic of the article is the economy, the impetus for the discussion was political. In this case, former Soviet Premier Nikita Khrushchev had just boastfully told this country that the Soviet Union would soon be richer than the United States —and got everybody worrying about how to get our economy moving faster.

The item that follows is a brief listing of the tools available to the Government to speed up economic growth: persuasion, monetary policy, or fiscal policy. And the final selection, by economist Emil Benoit, published in 1962, argues that of these tools the only appropriate one is an immediate tax reduction. As noted in the first section of this book, taxes were reduced in 1964 and 1965 and, as predicted, the nation's economic growth was stimulated.

## THE FEDERAL RESPONSIBILITY [1]

The securing of peace in the world and a high, stable level of employment at home are by common agreement the two crucial problems facing our times. On the first of these vital issues we have been witnessing the development of both national policy and international machinery that has the support of the great mass of Americans. But on the problem of maintaining full employment less progress has been made. Until recently the strident voices of extremists on the left and right still held the center of the stage with the result that there was no crystallization of national policy. The fact is, however, that we are not so bewildered as we seem and that the broad outlines of a program are taking shape, though much by way of clarification remains to be done.

By far the best vehicle for obtaining this clarification and for formulating a national full-employment policy is the Murray full-employment bill. While it is not very difficult to suggest improve-

[1] From "Toward Full Employment," by Milton Gilbert, an American economist currently affiliated with the Bank for International Settlements, Basle, Switzerland. *Fortune.* 32:158-9+. O. '45. Reprinted by permission of *Fortune* magazine; © 1945 Time Inc.

ments in the details of this proposed legislation, it is sound in purpose and in fundamentals. . . .

### Prevention of Depression Will Not Yield a Millennium But It Is the Prerequisite for Postwar Progress

To the large majority of Americans the specter of idle productive resources in the face of unsatisfied human wants has become intolerable. It is not only unemployment we resent, but empty factories, cold blast furnaces, and stalled machinery. And it is not that we don't appreciate and enjoy leisure but that we do not want leisure forced upon us when we would rather have the new radios, automobiles, and better houses that our capacity could make possible. Our basic economic problem is business depressions and how to prevent them.

In view of the extravagant claims that often creep into political debate, it must be emphasized from the start that preventing business from periodically going through the wringer will not usher in the millennium. The maintenance of full employment is not an assurance of perfect economic health. We have had in the past and will have in the future worries other than the alternating cycle of booms and depressions—the tariff, strikes, monopoly, inequality of income distribution, slums, and the question of public versus private ownership. Even in the best of worlds we cannot expect that no one will ever be unemployed or no business ever be short of orders under the dynamic conditions that surely lie ahead. Businessmen will not be suddenly possessed of perfect foresight, legislators imbued with unerring wisdom, or bureaucrats freed of red tape. Hence, not only must allowance be made for frictional unemployment, but we should count the job well done if we narrowly restrict the swings of the business cycle even though we do not wholly eliminate them.

What we do want to be sure of is that if business turns down something will be done before deflation spirals into disaster. If more than frictional unemployment exists, we want to have real assurance that the economic machine will not be allowed to settle into the rut of stagnation. Not to expect perfection but also not to tolerate complacency is the way the American voter will be able to judge leadership in this matter.

### The Objective of Full Employment Should Be Redefined in Terms of Business Sales That Match an Industrial Capacity

It must be admitted, too, that full employment is not a complete expression of our common objective. It allows too much debate about irrelevancies; it is loaded with the connotation of too many unacceptable, and often screwy, nostrums. I believe much of this would be avoided if it were recognized that full employment is only a symbol. Our objective could be more appropriately described, perhaps, as a level of business sales hovering in the neighborhood of effective business capacity. If sales are kept up to the level of business capacity to produce, we know the employment situation will be highly satisfactory.

Although capacity sales and full employment are in one sense opposite faces of the same coin, there is much to be gained by stressing the former rather than the latter term. It gives a better focus on both ends and means as a large number of us see them. Its overtones and implications force a consideration of the setting in which we want to work out any postwar unemployment problem. These implications must be made explicit before agreement on national policy can be reached, keeping in mind the proposition that sales equal markets, equal demand for production, equal jobs. The following points should be spelled out as the environment of our antidepression policy.

(1) A target of business sales consistent with effective productive capacity means that we intend to solve the business-cycle problem within the framework of the free-enterprise system of production. The jobs are not to be provided by government but by business. It is the role of government to assure a market for capacity output; it is the role of business to produce the goods and provide the jobs. The emphasis on business sales explicitly recognizes the benefits of business responsibility for production and the fact that those benefits are not to be sacrificed in seeking reasonable stability and security.

(2) It also means we are not dealing with a problem that is of concern only to labor or looking for a solution that will benefit only labor—as might be thought from the talk about full employment. Business depression concerns every group participating in the production process and sharing in the flow of national income arising from business sales. The counterpart of unemployment for labor is losses for enterprise.

(3) Furthermore, it means we are interested not in jobs that are a disguised dole but in work that will yield real value in terms of goods and services contributing to our standard of living. It conforms to the fact that real income is the objective, production the means, and that work is a cost.

(4) In addition, setting the goal in terms of business sales specifies that we do not want unemployment used as an excuse for the encroachment of government upon the areas of private production or government competition with business. Of course we know there is no hard and fast line separating the proper productive spheres of government and business. As our productive power increases we can surely expect to have better schooling as well as more automobiles, and we can expect that new areas of government service in such fields as health and social security will be developed along with the walkie-talkies and helicopters of the future. However, when industry is in the doldrums because of lack of demand, there is no reason to doubt its superior efficiency in producing automobiles and radios and no reason for government to invade such areas of production.

(5) Finally, by insisting that our objective is a high level of business sales, as well as full employment, we mean that all agents in the productive process—workers, farmers, managers, and investors—should earn their income by passing the test of usefulness in the market place. The government cannot guarantee everyone the specific job he wants any more than it can guarantee every business a high level of sales for the specific products it is making. It can see to it that demand in the market is active so that there are opportunities for the useful employment of labor and capital. But it must be up to the individual to adapt himself to those opportunities and to meet the requirements of the job, just as it must

be up to the businessman to produce what is wanted and to pass muster in the competitive system. As with all rights, the right to work—and its equivalent, the right to invest in and manage a business—implies responsibilities. We want the opportunities of an expanding economy; we don't want inefficiency propped up by paternalism.

### The Murray Bill Fixes Responsibility for Prosperous Economic Conditions Where It Belongs—in the Federal Government

All these points are already an integral part of the full-employment bill, and its congressional sponsors have invited any further clarification of language that may be needed. And having agreed upon maintaining the framework of the free-enterprise system, its motivations and disciplines, it will be possible to concentrate upon the essential provisions of the bill.

The first is that the *responsibility* for the maintenance of prosperous conditions be lodged in the government. This is where it belongs. The stark fact before us is that the next depression is now in the making. Several centuries of experience offer abundant proof that the free-enterprise system, left to itself, makes progress by alternating periods of booms and depressions. As the nation is now in the midst of a wartime boom, we can be sure that there is a depression coming up. There is, in fact, no dissent on this point, the only question at issue being when the depression will arrive. This means complete rejection of the extreme right-wing view, which appears to be that all would be fine if the conditions of the 1920's were reproduced in the postwar world. For this is what a program confined to low taxes, less government, and an environment favorable to business amounts to; we had them all in the twenties and yet that boom surely ushered in the thirties—and under the very best auspices.

The inevitable conclusion is that we cannot merely look backward. In the past the maintenance of economic stability was everybody's business but nobody's responsibility. Nonetheless, with characteristically sound instinct, the American people usually changed politicians when times were bad, not the business system. For the fact is that the only place in our economic and social system this responsibility can be fixed is in the national government. One may hope for economic developments so favorable that the government would have little to do to discharge its responsibility. One may debate about the ways and means by which this responsibility should be discharged by government. But on the essential point that maintaining prosperity is government's responsibility there should be no quibbling and can be no compromise. One of the merits of the full-employment bill is that it puts our political leaders on notice to that effect by proposing to enact this responsibility into law.

### The Murray Bill Provides Adequate Machinery for the Discharge of Government Responsibilities

There is a tendency to dodge this issue by directing attention to business planning for expansion. But after expansion comes contraction and all the business planning in the world will not stop it. The helplessness of the individual enterprise, large or small, caught in a deflationary spiral is all too familiar. Business cannot be antagonistic to government remedial action in such a situation because it has no substitute. To try to fix responsibility for remedial action on business is a perversion of the basic drive of private enterprise. When we accept the free-enterprise system, we must accept the profit motive as the guiding consideration in business decisions. We cannot impose social responsibilities on the individual business either to produce when there is no market or to hire labor when it has no need. Consequently, if something is to be done about depressions, government must do it. It is very well to insist that government create a climate favorable to business. However, it is equally important for business to create a climate favorable to necessary government action.

The second basic feature of the bill is the setting up of machinery for formulating government policies and programs. In this matter the bill leaves untouched the present division of functions between the administrative and legislative branches of the government. The President is directed to report to the Congress, no less frequently than once a year, on the state of the national economy and to present a definite program for curbing either deflationary or inflationary tendencies that may happen to prevail. The President can only advise and recommend; he cannot act without specific legislation provided by Congress.

The President's report and recommendations are to be received and considered by a new joint committee of the House and Senate, which will be responsible for the Federal budget and the government economic program as a whole. At the present time the various types of economic legislation are considered independently in a large number of specialized congressional committees with little opportunity for Congress itself to develop an integrated economic program with all its parts pointed in the same direction. Even the tax and expenditure sides of the Federal budget are handled by different committees. The President has a coordinating mechanism for securing consistency in his economic program through the Bureau of the Budget and the meetings of his Cabinet; the Congress should be organized to meet him on an equally integrated footing.

The establishment of a joint congressional committee would serve also to develop within Congress a group of experts on business-cycle problems. This group would gain the experience and be in a position to advise their congressional colleagues competently. As it is, Congress is not only lacking in organizational machinery but often finds it difficult to secure adequate knowledge of what is admittedly a difficult and technical subject.

### The Murray Bill Forces the Government to Assemble the Best Available Data on Current and Future Business Trends

As a third essential feature the full-employment bill provides that both the President and Congress cast up their appraisal of the business situation and measure the impact of remedial proposals in quantitative terms. It is safe to say that in no other way can the adequacy of the government's program or the desirability of alternative lines of action be judged.

The very calculation of total market demand would act against reliance on vague generalities, force into the open the reasoning behind proposed measures, and permit results to be checked after the event. It is necessary for the formation of an informed public opinion about economic matters and for assuring forthrightness in the discussion of economic problems.

The liberals can dream about four sugarplums if they will: the conservatives can insist upon four sour cherries if they must. But the basis for common understanding and compromise must be found in acceptance of the quantitative facts of economic life; they must be the point of departure in our efforts to make the business system function effectively.

The fact that this quantitative appraisal must be cast in terms of the prospective economic situation in order to serve as a guide to policy has made it one of the most criticized aspects of the bill. It is charged that accurate economic forecasting is impossible and that achieving the purposes of the bill is dependent upon accurate forecasting. There are two points to be made in this connection.

In the first place, the past few years have witnessed a major step forward in our knowledge of the workings of the business cycle. As recently as ten years ago the strategic factors in business fluctuations were much less clearly understood than they are today. One important result of the improvement in business-cycle theory has been a reorienting of the statistical work on national income and national product in a way that makes these statistics a much better tool for the analysis of the current and prospective economic situation. I believe that most of the business and government experts who have used this tool during the war are convinced of its adaptability to the national economic problems of the postwar period.

However that may be, it is even more important to recognize that the successful operation of a full-employment policy is not dependent upon accurate forecasting. What are needed are the current facts and current trends of the economic situation—employment and unemployment, business sales of the various goods and services, capital, investment, inventories, flow of production and income, and so on. Of course, in laying out future policy it is necessary and desirable that current known trends be projected into the somewhat unknown future. Not only the government but every business firm must make such projections to determine its purchasing, production, sales, and capital outlays programs for the year ahead. But they are required only as a working hypothesis—as a basis on which to proceed until known changes in conditions show that a change in operations is called for. This demonstrates, of course, that government policies and programs must be subject to change as business conditions change. But since frequent review of the applicability of the government's program to economic conditions is provided for in the bill, the criticism of the bill on this score is irrelevant.

### The Muray Bill Makes Government Spending a Means of Combating a Depression. It Is Conservative

Finally, the bill provides that if other ways and means cannot be found for assuring total market demand that will fully utilize the productive resources of the nation, the government's financial strength will be used to make good the deficiency in demand. Whether this financial support is to take the form of tax reduction, public works, increased social services, subsidies to investment or to consumption, or guaranteed loans either at home or abroad is left to future Congresses to decide, as it should be. But regardless of form, this commitment is the ultimate assurance that the business system will not be allowed to stall for lack of customers.

This does not mean that sole reliance is to be put upon government spending to offset fluctuations in business activity. It simply recognizes that all other means of correcting fundamental maladjustments in either the cost-price structure or the consumption-savings relationships are both slower acting and less certain in their results. The use of the fiscal instrument is required because it is the only instrument known to be effective within a relatively short period of time. It turned the tide in 1933 and again in 1938, and its effectiveness in mobilizing the full strength of our economy during the war is abundantly clear.

To some the use of the fiscal instrument seems a revolutionary change in our economic life. This is not the case. It is a new instrument, to be sure, but one that leaves the fundamental directives and arrangements of the free-enterprise system untouched. It recommends itself precisely because it is conservative in character. The only alternative to the indirect control of the business cycle, in which fiscal policy must be one of the instruments, is the direct control of the production and distribution machine—whether under government ownership or not. The indirect method can be utilized within the framework of the free enterprise system; the direct control of production implies a change in the system itself.

The use and consequences of fiscal policy can be illustrated by applying it to the depression of 1929-33. It will be recalled that during this period the annual total of consolidated business sales dropped from $93 billion to $48 billion, corporation profits of $7.2 billion were turned to a net loss of $3.6 billion, while unemployment rose to staggering proportions. Of course much could have been done to lessen the severity of the deflationary sweep— the gyrations of the sterling-dollar rate of exchange or the collapse of the banking system could have been prevented, to mention only the most obvious things. But suppose all such measures had proved unavailing and it had been decided that the only way to stop the downward drift of business was through a government-expenditure program. How much would it have cost and what would have been its effect?

It can be readily calculated that to maintain business sales and the flow of national income at their 1929 levels through the years 1930 to 1933 would have required no more than $25 billion of government expenditures for the entire period. The government would have had only to enter the market as any other buyer and purchase $25 billion worth of goods, timed so as to offset the decline in private purchases, and business would have done the rest. No control of business need have been imposed; consumers could have had complete freedom of choice; free choice of job selection by labor need not have been abridged; no government competition with business was necessary. These government expenditures would have resulted in consolidated business sales more than $125 billion higher for the four-year period and business earnings, excluding farm enterprises, $45 billion larger than was actually the case. The cost to the government would have been only about half the cost of the depression to business in terms of profits alone, not to mention the bankruptcies, the foreclosed homes and farms, and the cost in human misery of mass unemployment.

The reason these government expenditures would have had such large results is that they would have headed off the deflationary spiral in which declining investment leads to declining employment, payrolls, and consumption, and declining consumption in turn further reduces investment. Thus the government spending would not only have directly provided a market for business output but would indirectly have maintained the flow of income to consumers and the flow of consumer buying. Furthermore, heading off the deflationary spiral in this way would have prevented the drastic inventory liquidation and the negative net capital expenditures by business that actually occurred. Government spending could not have depressed private capital investment further because there was virtually none by 1932. As a matter of fact, had government spending been used, the collapse of business, and with it the demoralization of business confidence, would have been avoided. The level of business investment would have been substantially higher than it was in the years 1930-1933, even though it was sure to be lower than at the peak in 1929. The fact is that it is cheaper and easier to stay out of a depression than to get out of one that is allowed to impose deflation on the whole economy.

With our streets and highways far from adequate for modern needs, with the need for better schools and hospitals, with the vast opportunities for regional development, there is no question but that this $25 billion could have been wisely spent for useful public improvements that would have contributed to our standard of living and yet been noncompetitive with private business. And in the meanwhile there would have been opportunity to correct the fundamental disturbances in the economic mechanism and to get over the temporary saturation of the capital-goods market so that the government expenditure program could have been tapered off.

*The Use of Fiscal Policy Requires No Greater Statesmanship Than the United States Will Need in Other Spheres*

These, then, are the elements of a workable full-employment policy. They are not the whole story, but the rest must be worked out in accordance with the requirements and possibilities of unfolding economic conditions. They should be retained in the refined and clarified full-employment and *full-production* bill now before Congress.

Of the opposing arguments that have not been touched on above, either explicitly or implicitly, the characteristic that stands out is the surprising distrust of the quality of our statesmanship. It is said, for example, that the economic program of Congress will be dictated by sectional or group interests rather than by the needs of the economic situation. Our experience does not reveal this to be a serious objection, even granting that the democratic process necessarily involves give and take. Or it is contended that the government expenditure program will lead to inflation. As the objective of such a program is specified to be combating deflation, this contention can imply only that Congress and the President will be unable to read the facts correctly as to when a change in program is necessary. Or it is charged that full employment will strengthen labor's hand in demanding impossibly high wages, resulting in continuous inflation. But it is evident that the power of any special interest group is subsidiary to the power of Congress and that it can be strictly limited whenever the public interest requires.

Because of fears such as these, we are sometimes urged to trim our sails in advance, to limit the government's responsibility to the prevention of mass unemployment instead of embracing in it the positive assurance of full production and employment. But to set our sights on half a loaf is unacceptable on two scores. In the first place, it is offensive to logic. Either we know what to do about unemployed economic resources or we do not. And if we do, it makes no sense to say that action can and should be taken to reduce (potential) unemployment from twelve million to six million but that nothing further should be done to reduce the six to three.

Moreover, it represents a serious misreading of the temper of the times. The world is not willing to admit that the economic machine created by man cannot be made to serve the needs of all men. It is only trying to decide whether free enterprise or socialism is the more promising road. As surely as the attempt at the San Francisco Conference to circumscribe the goal of full employment in the United Nations Charter was voted down, so will this nation sacrifice its role of world leadership if it fails to take a positive stand on this matter. If the United States, with its great resources and its record of achievement under capitalism, cannot believe that the job can be done under the free-enterprise system, no one else will. Only the objective of full production and employment is in keeping with the high ideals of our tradition—that the United States is the land of freedom, opportunity, and plenty.

## THE CONSUMER AS KING [2]

### Phase One: The Progressive Period, 1901-16

First, a few words about the progressive period; that is, the period from, roughly, the accession of Theodore Roosevelt in 1901 to the engulfment of Woodrow Wilson's Administration in the problems of the First World War.

Although McKinley had easily won the election of 1900, with a stance that looked backward to the sequence of Republican administrations which had dominated the drive to maturity after the Civil War, American life in a wider sense had been actively preparing itself for a shift in the balance of its objectives; and this was revealed by the popularity of Theodore Roosevelt's style and rhetoric, as well as by the clear-cut bipartisan defeat of Taft, and all he then appeared to represent, in the election of 1912.

The progressive objectives had, then, fifteen years of relative dominance over domestic policy; and they left their mark. By 1916 the United States had accepted the most revolutionary of all forms of economic policy, the progressive income tax; it had created a climate in which big business curbed itself or was, to a degree, curbed; the unions were given explicitly the right to organize, outside the Anti-Trust Act; a Federal Reserve System was created, in part to permit a degree of public control to be exercised over the trade cycle. In some of the states even more powerful measures of social control were introduced. But the progressive period was more a matter of mood and the direction of policy than of drastic reallocation of resources.

[2] From *Stages of Economic Growth*, by W. W. Rostow, economist and adviser to the Johnson Administration. Cambridge University Press. New York. '60. p 75-81. Reprinted by permission.

In these years Americans made another significant decision about the direction of national affairs. In the 1890's a widespread mood was generating that the United States had, in some sense, become a mature world power, and that it was time for it to play a major role on the world scene; to move out from behind the protective barrier represented by the Monroe Doctrine and the implicit deal with the British, in which the British navy shielded the United States from the vicissitudes of the Eurasian balance-of-power game. And Theodore Roosevelt, architect of the seizure of the Philippines and hero of the Spanish-American War, pressed forward this sense of emergence and, to a degree, of assertion on the world scene in his two Administrations.

But the so-called "large view" symbolized by Theodore Roosevelt failed to take hold. The Philippines were kept; but Americans, having been tempted, and fallen a bit from what they conceived to be isolationist grace, in the end turned their backs on the acquisition of empire. In foreign policy they opted for a version of the British Liberal rather than the British Conservative tradition, in the progressive period—quite explicitly so in the figure of Wilson.

American resources, then, did not flow in significantly increased volume either to social services or to military outlays; although the progressive legislation, the Great White Fleet [a 1907-1908 Atlantic to Pacific naval cruise by sixteen battleships and four destroyers], and the increased role of government in American society were facts.

American resources did, however, flow increasingly into the third post-maturity alternative—into new dimensions of consumption: a trend damped by the rise in urban living costs down to 1920, but palpable in the next major phase, that is, in the boom of the 1920's.

### Phase Two: The 1920's

The American 1920's are generally now studied as a period of tragic isolation; as the prelude to severe depression; or as a bizarre social era of bathtub gin, jazz, mah jong, glamorous athletes, distinguished novelists, and the Charleston.

But that decade is also to be understood as the first protracted period in which a society absorbed the fruits and consequences of the age of durable consumers' goods and services.

Let us examine now a few figures which suggest the character of the change proceeding in American society, and in its economy, over this era of high mass-consumption of which the 1920's is the centerpiece.

First, there was the rise of a new middle class. Between 1900 and 1940 the number of farmers in the United States declined. Those in manufacture, construction, and transport—including skilled workers—rose about in proportion to the total rise in the working force. But semiskilled workers increased more than twice as rapidly as the working force as a whole; professional people and office workers three times as rapidly as the working force as a whole. The era of the professional technician, and of the skilled and semiskilled worker had come; and this trend in the structure of the working force has proved virtually universal to all post-maturity societies.

Now where did this population, oriented increasingly towards the provision and enjoyment of consumers' goods and services, live? The answer is that the population was not only increasingly urban, but increasingly suburban. In the 1920's the American population as a whole increased by 16 per cent. Those living in the centers of cities increased by 22 per cent. But those living in the satellite areas—the suburbs—increased by 44 per cent.

What then happened to manufacturing output? [The economist Dr. Solomon] Fabricant has arrayed the increases in physical output in the United States between 1899 and 1937 by order of increase. Automobiles lead the list with an increase of 180,100 per cent; cigarettes, petroleum, milk, beetsugar are all over 1000 per cent; cement, canned fruits and vegetables are only a little under 1000 per cent.

What does all this add up to? The United States took to wheels. This was quite truly the age of the mass automobile. With the automobile the United States began a vast inner migration into newly constructed, single-family houses in the suburbs; and these new houses were filled increasingly with radios, refrigerators, and the other household gadgetry of a society whose social mobility and productivity had all but wiped out personal service. Within these houses Americans shifted their food consumption to higher-grade foods, increasingly purchased in cans—or, later, frozen.

Automobiles, single-family houses, roads, household durables, mass markets in higher-grade foods—these tell a good deal of the story of the transformation of American society in the 1920's, a transformation which supported the boom of the 1920's and which altered the whole style of a continent's life, down to its courting habits.

*Phase Three: The Great Depression*

Then came, of course, a decade's severe and protracted depression. We shall not consider at length here the causes of the onset of depression or the reasons for its extraordinary depth, except to say this much: in its onset, the depression of 1929 was a perfectly normal cyclical down-turn; the leading sectors of the boom were wearing a little thin, notably in housing, stimulated by the housing back-log built up during the First World War, but weakened by the deceleration in population growth and family formation. The depression went abnormally deep because the institutions of credit, at home and abroad, broke down, like a series of collapsing floors, grinding the cycle at each stage of collapse to a lower point, through its effects on income, confidence, and expectations.

The length of the depression in the United States—as opposed to its depth—deserves rather more comment; for it relates directly to the stage of growth, to the era of high mass-consumption, into which the United States had entered.

Although many ancillary forces undoubtedly played a part, the central reason for the intractability of the American depression, which still left 17 per cent unemployed on the eve of the Second World War, was that the leading sectors of this phase of American growth required full employment and an atmosphere of confidence before they could become activated again.

What were those leading sectors in the American age of high consumption? They were, once again, the automobile, suburban home-building, road-building, and the progressive extension of the automobile and other durable consumers' goods to more and more families. When, in earlier historical stages, the momentum of growth hinged on the continued extension of railroads, or on the introduction of other cost-reducing industrial processes—on the side of supply—investment could be judged profitable at relatively low levels of current consumers' demand. But when investment comes to be centered around industries and services based on expanding consumption, full employment is needed, in a sense, to sustain full employment; for unless consumption levels press outward, capacity in consumers' goods industries and those supplying them with inputs will be underused, and the impulse to invest will be weak. The horizons of American industry lowered radically in the 1930's, and appeared almost to stabilize at a low level.

When, in the nineteenth century, steel went mainly into railways or the new steel ships, the demand for steel was a reflex of what some economists like to call exogenous investment; in the age of high consumption, when the demand for steel is, let us say, from the automobile firms and canning industries, the demand for steel becomes a reflex of endogenous investment—of the rise of incomes, of the accelerator, one may say.

On this view the Second World War was a sort of *deus ex machina* which brought the United States back up to full employment; and in the context of the postwar world—its institutional arrangements drastically altered by the New Deal and such legislation as that put through for veterans' housing—the United States went on to round out the durable consumers' goods revolution in a decade of chronic full employment between, say, 1946 and 1956.

During the depression, American society did more, of course, than merely experience a depression. When the engine of growth based on the automobile, suburbia, and durable consumers' goods broke down, the United States threw its weight hard towards a postmaturity alternative, that is, to increased allocations for social welfare purposes. And the contours of the welfare state were rounded out under Franklin Roosevelt to remain an accepted part of the American scene, down to the present.

## Phase Four: The Postwar Boom

The fourth phase—the great postwar boom of 1946-56—can be regarded as a resumption of the boom of the 1920's. The march to the outer suburbs continued after a marked deceleration in the 1930's. In 1948, 54 per cent of American families owned their own cars; a decade later, 73 per cent. In 1946, 69 per cent of houses wired for electricity had electric refrigerators; a decade later the figure was 96 per cent; and the figures for other electric gadgets— for example, the vacuum cleaner and electric washer—are similar. Television was installed in 86 per cent of such homes by 1956.

And although the deep-freeze and air conditioning are just beginning to take hold in American households it is clear that American growth can no longer continue to be based so heavily on the extension to a higher and higher proportion of the community of the suburban house, the automobile, and the standard mix of electric-powered gadgets. In some items output began to fall off absolutely before the recent recession when the automobile industry, seized of *hybris* in its recent models, overreached itself and was suddenly forced to learn that all sectoral growth curves are subject to long-run deceleration. (This transition poses, incidentally, an interesting problem for the United States; for it occurs at just the time when Western Europe, Japan, and—some distance behind —Russia, are entering a rapid-growth stage in durable consumers' goods. Some important part of the American export advantage in recent times has been based on its pioneering status in these light-engineering commodities. Now they are being mass-produced efficiently in many countries, where lower wage rates prevail. Is Detroit repeating a version of what British manufacturers of cotton goods and rail iron went through in the more distant past?)

### Phase Five: Where Next?

What then does the future hold? Are Americans, having fashioned this suburban, mobile civilization going to settle down to tidy it up a little, and enjoy the benefits of affluence? Is it the four-day work week and the three-day weekend which is coming soon? Some think it is; and it is still too soon dogmatically to deny their judgment.

But it is clear that something new and important did happen in American society as the age of durable consumers' goods moved towards its logical conclusion. . . . As the durable consumers' goods revolution was moving to a point where the rate of diffusion had to slow down, American society made a most extraordinary and unexpected decision. Americans began to behave as if they preferred the extra baby to the extra unit of consumption.

During the war years the birth rate rose from 18 per 1000 to about 22. This was judged at the time—and to a large degree it certainly was—a phenomenon of resumed full employment and early wartime marriages. In the postwar years, however, the level of births moved up and stayed at about 25 per 1000, yielding a rise in the population, as well as changes in the age-structure of the population and in the rate of family formation, of major economic significance. An official forecast of American population made in 1946 estimated that the American population would reach 165 million in 1990; that figure was, in fact, passed within a decade. At the moment American population is increasing at a rate of more than 1.5 per cent *per annum,* and is predicted to be some 240 million by 1980.

This reimposition of Malthusianism in American society, in all its consequences, combined with other circumstances—notably the cumulative deficit in social overhead capital and the cost of the arms race, if it should continue—are likely to make the next decade in American history one of vigorous expansion of output, touched at the level of private consumption by a degree of austerity.

To make this notion of strain on private consumption more concrete consider an estimate of the "dependency ratio" recently calculated in a study of American population by Conrad and Irene Taeuber. That ratio measures the relation between the working population and those outside the working-force age limits—in the United States those under twenty and over sixty-five. It is calculated in the form of the number of dependent persons one hundred members of the working force must support. Historically that ratio has been falling; that is, each member of the working force has had to support fewer and fewer persons outside. In 1915 it was 84; in 1935, as low as 74; but by 1955 it had risen back to 81; and on the basis of present population structure and birth rates it will be of the order of 98 in 1975.

In short, by its own choice, American society as of 1959 is not quite as affluent as it looks. It is too soon for a four-day week and for tolerance of substantial levels of unemployment, if only the unemployment benefits are large enough—as Professor Galbraith has counseled. A society like the United States, structurally committed to a high-consumption way of life; committed also to maintain the decencies that go with adequate social overhead capital; committed by its own interests and the interests of those dependent upon it or allied to it to deal with a treacherous and extremely expensive world environment; committed additionally, out of its own internal dynamics, to a rapidly enlarging population and to a working force which must support more old and more young . . . such a society must use its resources fully, productively, and wisely. The problem of choice and allocation—the problem of scarcity—has not yet been lifted from it.

## GROW WE MUST [3]

Western interest in growth tends, like the Western economy, to fluctuate. Last year when growth in Europe seemed to be slowing down and growth in America and Britain refused to speed up, voices were raised warning the West that general stagnation and decline might lie ahead.

This year, apart from some concern about the level of industrial investment, Europe seems to have recovered its confidence. Britain is consciously set on expansion. The American economy seems to be "moving" again. So the anxieties have lessened. Yet concern will return at the least sign of flagging confidence. In any case, too, the disparity in rates of growth between various groups of countries is so great that the subject is interesting in itself, quite apart from its more apocalyptic implications.

In simplest terms, the debate about growth concerns this question: On what scale should a society add, each year, to its existing stock of goods and services? Is the average expansion of 2.5 per cent of national income registered in Britain and America for the past eight years enough? Or should economies aim at the 5 to 6 per cent rate of growth of Western Europe? Or the 7 to 8 per cent

[3] From "The West Debates the Great Growth Issue," by Barbara Ward. New York *Times Magazine.* p 22+. O. 27, '63. © 1963 by The New York Times Company. Reprinted by permission. Barbara Ward (Lady Jackson) is a British economist of international reputation and author of *The Rich Nations and the Poor Nations* and other books.

claimed by the Communists? Or the fabulous 10 per cent actually achieved by the Japanese?

The question of more rapid growth is a new one in world politics. For millennia it never arose. All human societies were trapped in the subsistence economy in which the outer limits were fixed by available land and water. Once population reached those limits, declining output, fragmentation of holdings, starvation, banditry and war drove the population back to a level the land could support. It was from this universal trap of the subsistence economy that Western science and technology rescued mankind.

Today the essence of the effort for growth made by the developing nations is to follow the Western world and Russia out of the subsistence age of static agriculture and marginal industry into the infinitely wider opportunities of modern technology in all its forms. Those developing nations are still short of everything —savings, skills, markets. They are on the bottom rungs of the ladder of modernization, where problems of supply dominate every aspect of the economy. Their need to grow is absolute, for growth alone conquers shortages.

But if the need for developing economies to grow as rapidly as they can is obvious, what of the fully modernized states? So rich already, do they need to become still richer, and to become so faster? An average citizen of India subsisting on $60 a year can hardly fail to want more. But an average American family income is over $5,000 a year. What, in such a context, is the argument for more rapid expansion?

The first point to be made is that rich nations are, after all, not uniformly rich; both Italy and the United States have their Deep Souths. Secondly, rich countries do not entirely escape the dilemmas of a growing population and rising unemployment, as more adolescents arrive in the labor market and automation steadily cuts the demand for unskilled and semiskilled labor. If, as in America, many of these youths are colored, really explosive dangers begin to build up.

Another point: If the poorer countries are to grow, they must sell, at a reasonably high price, to the richer nations, and the prices they get for their primary produce—cocoa, coffee, tin, tea—

depend on prosperity in the developed West. If the West settled down to, say, a steady 5 per cent rate of expansion, primary prices could find a rather higher level than the still generally depressed prices of today. And higher prices would do more to underpin sustained development than any Western aid or investment.

At the same time, an expanding West depends on a steady increase in markets. For Western markets gradually reach saturation. In a real sense, the growth of the developing nations is an important precondition of sustained economic buoyancy in the West.

Perhaps the best route toward a solution to the whole growth problem is to look at the developed economies during their most recent period of rapid expansion and ask whether they had anything in common at that point. One can take Japan and Western Europe in almost any year since 1955 and examine Britain and America before 1954. What their economies shared in their years of rapid growth was, above all, one thing—*a high level of demand, sustained when necessary by the actions of government.*

The jump in arms spending for the Korean war, coupled with the final phase of postwar restocking, gave America its last experience of demand high enough to employ, even overemploy, all its resources. A similar, though lesser, boost gave Britain's Conservative government two or three years of "Tory prosperity."

In the countries of high growth rates, one can observe a combination of high private and public demand similar to that of the United States during the Korean war. The private demand comes from the surge toward consumer durables, the public demand from the readiness of governments to pump, whenever necessary, more demand into the economy, either by direct public spending or indirectly by tax reliefs—both routes leading, temporarily, to an unbalanced budget.

Proof that governments in developed countries can increase the rate of growth by creating a greater urgency of demand is to be found quite simply in the West's experience of the war economy. In four short years—between 1940 and 1944—the United States doubled the size of its industrial base. So large was the expansion that civilian standards could increase in spite of the overwhelming concentration on arms, and the postwar economy started at a new high level of capital equipment.

Nor is the proof only to be found in Western experience. In one sense, any achievement the Soviets have to show in rapid growth springs from the fact that they virtually treat their economy as a war economy, with a vast governmental program voraciously ordering the capital goods for further expansion.

In fact, the evidence for the belief that governments, at least in large and developed lands, can stimulate growth by stimulating demand is so generally accepted that not wild-eyed radicals but sober working parties attached to the Atlantic Community's Organization for Economic Cooperation and Development have stated dogmatically their belief that sustained demand is *the* key to growth and governments can put their hands on the key.

At this point, some people may begin to wonder what all the fuss is about. We need growth. Demand stimulates it. Governments can stimulate demand. Then why not cut the debate and get on with the stimulus?

The matter is not, however, so straightforward and painless. In fact, there are two major hurdles to be overcome—at least in the West. The first is the risk of inflation; the second is the risk of creating an "overmighty" state.

Neither risk can be shrugged off. In economies operating at a high level of activity the historical tendency is, at least in the short run, for all resources to become scarce and for their prices to rise. If industrialists are all bidding for labor and materials, the cost of both goes up. At some point, they begin their squeeze on profits and hence on the capital accumulated through profits. At some further point, falling profits lead to lower investment and a general reduction in activity. Such was the pattern of the old-fashioned boom and bust.

But the busts at least lowered prices. If, in the future, it is to be all boom and no bust, may not steadily rising prices finally lead to deepening inflation, undermine all confidence in the currency and thus lead in the end to a worse crash by a rather longer route?

Nor should one forget the international repercussions. If trading and exporting nations allow their costs to go uncontrollably up, other nations' goods will be more competitive. Imports will increase, exports will decline and the economy, like a horse too sharply reined in, will be pulled back on its heels by vanishing reserves and a balance-of-payments crisis. One reason for Britain's semithrottled condition in recent years has been the speed with which domestic expansion has led first to inflation and then to a flight from sterling.

Yet the answer cannot be to clamp down on all wage increases, since rising wages are the *chief* means of keeping demand in step with the fabulous productivity of the new technologies—our new machines in fact threaten to turn us all into sorcerer's apprentices watching helplessly while our markets are flooded with rising output.

The second fear—of increasing and excessive government regulation—has fewer facts to support it. No developed community has slipped into total regimentation by small, cumulative steps. Communism has triumphed only in relatively underdeveloped societies and usually by force in a coup d'état. Fascism imposed its control on developed nations in a state of crisis brought on, in Germany at least, not by too much government intervention but by the massive and prolonged unemployment resulting from too little.

Yet one can still admit in theory that steady state stimulus to demand could bring about so intricate an involvement of government in every aspect of business that the free economy, as we know it, would be no more. Soviet planning, which is usually what people have in mind as a horrific norm, does entail just such interventions. Its example suggests that a wholly state-directed economy without alternative sources of employment and decision-making would be a very uncertain base for political freedom.

In fact, no Western advocate of more rapid growth seeks such complete intervention. But the fears exist. Before, therefore, one can determine the prospects for growth in the relatively unregulated economies of the West, these two formidable objections have to be met.

To begin with inflation, probably the decisive element in the postwar variety has been the pressure of wages, revised upward almost every year, on industrial costs and hence on prices. Where, as in Germany until 1960, labor bargainers felt the restraints imposed by memories of catastrophic inflation in the past and by the current arrival of thousands of refugee workers from East Germany, there was little pressure for large wage increases. Expansion without inflation—of the order of 6 and 7 per cent a year—could go ahead. But in recent years, German labor costs have gone up by about 40 per cent and cries of alarm echo from Bonn and from business. In France, too, the threat of inflation has become very real, and the government has recently moved to meet it.

What is needed is not a general check on all wages but a rate of wage increase which on the average—some expanding industries paying more, some contracting industries paying less—does not exceed the community's annual capacity to produce more goods. The level might be 3 per cent in some years, higher in others. Fully employed economies need, in fact, some agreed norm to which the wage bill could be related.

Britain's new National Incomes Commission is designed to set such a standard. The wage level is regularly discussed by the French Planning Commission. Sweden and Holland have even achieved a measure of national agreement by way of discussions between employers and unions. Thus the theory of a steady and reasonable increase in wages contained within certain agreed annual limits is already known. Occasionally it is acted on. But no one can pretend that it is widely understood or that labor unions are quick to accept the reasoning behind it.

Nor is their acceptance made easier by the general divorce of workers from any direct share in profits or by the fantastic rewards —in stock options and so forth—which some businesses shower on senior executives. Restraint cannot, in a democratic society, be preached to one section of the community alone.

To turn now to the political risk of regimentation, here a more positive answer can be given. In the last decade, several countries have developed wholly new techniques of economic planning and forecasting and their calculations, based upon the computer and upon input-output analysis, promise to make available to society, *without* oppressive regulation, a sense of scope and direction which could wholly transform the businessman's sense of opportunity—

and it is, after all, on this that in large measure growth in free economies depends.

The French, gently prodded by Jean Monnet, have led the way. Their Planning Commission examines with business leaders and trade unionists the implications for the economy of, say, a 4 or a 5 per cent rate of growth—the demand it postulates for power, for steel, for transport, for machine tools. With this picture of buoyant demand before their eyes, businessmen go away and take the decisions on investment consonant with such a rate of growth—and their decisions are a key factor in ensuring that the rate occurs.

The Japanese use a comparable technique in plotting budgetary policy. For some years the government made an annual estimate of the amount of growth the Japanese economy was likely to achieve in the next twelve months. Then another estimate was made on what additional tax revenues would be earned by the extra production. A sum equivalent to those potential revenues was then remitted in tax relief and became available for spending in the economy. The stimulus thus given proved one of the chief ways in which the next surge of growth was secured.

Belgium has acted to create a planning mechanism, Spain and Italy are considering it, Britain and Canada are setting up national economic development councils as a first step. For years, private firms have, of course, used detailed analysis and forecasting for their own market surveys. The new technique is largely an adaptation of the procedures to national markets. It does not imply detailed regulation. It does give an impetus and momentum to private choice and public plans.

We may thus conclude that free society in the West is beginning to evolve new answers to the new problems created by the pressing need to secure higher rates of growth. As in every period of creative change, many minds do not accept either the new needs or the new policies designed to meet them. In the United States—but very much less in Europe—a rigid orthodoxy still prevails on most matters concerning governments and their interventions in the economy. Many of the techniques now used in Western Europe or Japan to keep demand high and buoyant—flexible budgeting (which may include deficit financing in slack years), forecasting and indicative planning agencies, attempts to construct an acceptable strategy for wages—all these are denounced as dangerous departures from the accepted way of doing things.

Arguments to counter such dogmatism cannot be marshaled easily, for emotion as well as reason is involved. Yet it is a sobering thought that thirty-four years ago—when budgets were small and generally balanced, when unions were unorganized and taxes low, when business did its own forecasting and the market reigned supreme—in short, at a time of very considerable laissez-faire, there occurred an almost total collapse of demand in Western markets which in turn introduced the worst depression in the history of capitalism.

Today, there are enough uncertainties in the West—slower investment in Europe, unemployment in America, low income among the primary producers—to suggest that the buoyant growth of the last decade, which has put communism more or less on the defensive all around the world, cannot be relied on simply to maintain itself unaided. If all new policies for growth are rejected, may not the old policies lead back to the old result—the collapse of demand, the disarray of the West, the resurgence of extremism?

This is the general context within which policies for growth must be considered. In such a perspective, it is not easy, rationally, to dismiss problems simply because they wear an unfamiliar face, or to refuse policies which, being designed to meet new problems, are themselves still new.

## IS THE NATION GROWING FAST ENOUGH? [4]

Between now and 1970, predicted Nikita Khrushchev recently, the Soviet Union will catch and then pass the United States as the world's foremost economic power. Russian output will race ahead, he said, at the rate of 8.6 per cent annually; the United States is poking along at less than 2 per cent. Khrushchev's brassy boast is open to doubt: the United States puts out accurate figures, but no one can vouch for the Russian "percentages." The real question is whether the United States is growing fast enough, not just to stay ahead of Russia, but for its own economic well-being.

[4] From article in *Time.* 73:90. F. 16, '59. Courtesy *Time;* Copyright Time Inc. 1959.

Judged by unemployment alone, the United States is not. Industrial production is back almost to peak levels, and yet industry still has 20 per cent unused capacity, along with 4,108,000 unemployed (6.1 per cent of the labor force). There are other doubts about economic growth. After half a century of expansion at an average 3 per cent annually, the real United States gross national product (excluding price boosts) has gained only an average 1.3 per cent annually over the last five years.

Administration economists profess not to be worried. The real, noninflated gain in GNP for 1953 was 4.4 per cent, that for 1955 a fat 8 per cent. What knocked the average off was a minus 1.9 per cent in the 1954 recession and a minus 3.2 per cent last year. Says one top-level Washington economist: "The boys who average these things out catch us at the low end of the cycle. If you judged 1959 and 1960 in over-all terms, we would have nothing to worry about."

To judge the constantly changing, increasingly complex U.S. economy solely by GNP is also a risky business. Much of the slowdown in the rate of gain between 1952 and 1958 can be attributed to slowing in industrial production of hard goods. But consumers bought so many other things that the volume of consumer buying kept growing an average 3.5 per cent annually, well above the 3 per cent "norm." The continuing consumer demand means that production—and thus GNP—must take another jump.

Nevertheless, almost every economist from New Dealing Leon Keyserling to the Rockefeller Brothers Fund experts and Harvard's Sumner Slichter would like to see the United States grow faster. They agree that the old 3 per cent target is outdated and that the goal should be 5 per cent a year from now on.

The argument is chiefly over how to achieve the 5 per cent: by massive Government help or the resources of private industry? AFL-CIO economist Stanley Ruttenberg would like the Government to do much more of the job. He wants a loosening of credit, a big (and probably unbalanced) budget, with huge Federal school, housing and other programs to make full employment. What about inflation? No problem, say the spenders. . . .

Others, including Harvard's Slichter, White House Economic Adviser Raymond Saulnier, and the Federal Reserve's William

McChesney Martin have different ideas on growth. They argue that force-feeding offers no assurance of healthy growth, and point to the fact that all the spending and big deficits of the 1930's did not lick the depression. On the contrary, the United States had its two most prosperous years—1956 and 1957—when the budget ran a surplus.

From such facts Martin and other experts argue that the best way to expand is to improve the economic climate, so that business-men will have the incentive to accomplish greater growth them-selves. They want to work toward a balanced budget, not merely for the symmetrical sake of balance itself, but in order to cut taxes as an encouragement to both business and consumers. Even the AFL-CIO's Ruttenberg admits that tax cuts "worked" when the Administration chopped taxes $7.5 billion in 1954: the next year's growth was 8 per cent. How to cut taxes and still maintain vitally important defense programs? Economist Slichter thinks it is just a matter of "common sense," starting with the $5.3 billion farm sub-sidy. Says Slichter: "The farm subsidies are just plain corruption."

Businessmen would also like to see a more realistic depreciation policy. United States Steel estimates that between 1940 and 1956 the difference between depreciation allowances and the actual re-placement cost of equipment was $904 million.

The most convincing argument against Government Interven-tion is the industrial lessons of the last few years. Booms in hi-fi, boating, photography, travel, frozen and gourmet foods, all come from relatively new things that tempted consumers to part with their cash. This is the real road to growth, the innovation of exciting and useful new products and industries that Government alone cannot start. It can only provide the incentive for business to im-prove itself. As Harvard's Slichter says: "You can't expand without demand for the product. We need less sales talk, less hot air and better quality and more originality."

## THE TOOLS AT HAND [5]

The Federal Government, over the past half-century, has as-sumed an ever larger role in managing the United States economy.

[5] From "Maintenance of Prosperity," by Richard L. Worsnop, staff writer. *Editorial Research Reports.* 2, no 21:902-4. D. 2, '66. Reprinted by permission.

As Federal spending and tax revenues have risen, so has Washington's power to stimulate or retard national economic growth. In addition, the Federal Reserve Board's control of monetary policy exerts a powerful influence on the availability of money and credit.

## Federal Reserve's Weapons of Monetary Policy

Of the tools used by the Federal Reserve to influence the level of economic activity, perhaps the best known is the discount rate. Changes in the discount rate must be made separately by each of the twelve district Federal Reserve banks. Usually, though, all Reserve banks act at about the same time, and in practice the rates are raised or lowered upon the initiative of the Board of Governors of the Federal Reserve System. [The discount rate is the rate of interest charged by Federal Reserve banks in their dealings with commercial and other banks.—Ed.]

The discount rate generally is used by the Board to signal a shift in the direction of policy. If it is raised, interest rates—particularly those on short-term loans—usually rise and credit tightens. Conversely, a cut in the discount rate ordinarily is followed by easier conditions in the money and capital markets. What an increase in the discount rate does is to put a brake on borrowing from the Reserve by member banks, and as the member banks pass along the higher rate to their customers, there is a brake on borrowing all along the line.

The monetary tool with the most immediate and widespread impact is the Board's power to vary member bank reserve requirements. A change in reserve requirements alters the ratio of cash reserves that member banks must keep in relation to their deposits. Lowering the reserve requirements has the effect of making more of a bank's money available for lending, and raising it has the reverse effect.

## Operation of Fiscal Policy in American Economy

Fiscal policy, which sometimes runs counter to monetary policy, has to do with the exercise of Federal taxation and spending powers. When tax revenues exceed expenditures, money is drawn out of the economy, thus producing a deflationary effect. When spending surpasses tax receipts, inflationary pressure increases because of the additional money injected into the economy.

Conventional economic wisdom holds that the Federal Government, in time of recession, should cut spending in an effort to balance its budget. But Heller and other advocates of the New Economics maintain that just the opposite course should be followed. They contend that a recession should be met by increased Government spending, even at the risk of incurring a substantial budget deficit. When recovery comes, it is argued, tax receipts will increase sufficiently to offset whatever deficit was required to get the economy moving forward.

The trouble with this reasoning is that legislation to increase or decrease taxes, or to raise or reduce appropriations, ordinarily takes months to make its way through Congress. By the time it is ready for approval, the economic climate may have changed and the legislative remedy may thus appear too harsh or too mild.

Persuasion is still another weapon in the government's economic arsenal. The wage-price guideposts, first enunciated in the 1962 Economic Report of the Council of Economic Advisers, afford the most notable recent example of Federal efforts to control inflation by voluntary means. The general guide for . . . [wages] was that "the percentage increase in total compensation per man-hour be equal to the national trend-rate of increase in output per manhour." The price guidepost called for "stable prices in industries enjoying the same productivity growth as the average of the economy; rising prices in industries with smaller than average productivity gains; and declining prices in industries with greater than average productivity gains."

## THE CASE FOR A TAX CUT [6]

Ex-President Hoover has just expressed sympathy for President Kennedy. He remembers all too well what it is like to assume office shortly before a major stock market break, and with a basical-

[6] From "A Tax Cut Now?" by Emile Benoit. *New Republic*. 147:15-19. Ag. 13, '62. Reprinted by permission of *The New Republic*, © 1962, Harrison-Blaine of New Jersey, Inc. Emile Benoit is Professor of International Business at the Columbia Graduate School of Business. He was formerly economic attaché with the United States embassies in London and Vienna.

ly unsympathetic Congress to work with. It would be ironical indeed if a President elected on the pledge to get a nation moving again was destined to repeat Mr. Hoover's tragicomedy of indecision and inaction in the face of a softening of the U.S. economy.

This softening is now widely admitted, but there is a paralysis of the will to act. Though we are far from achieving the production and employment goals of the Employment Act of 1946, we are still "waiting for more evidence"; and each month we wait costs us $2 to $3 billions of extra goods and services the nation badly needs and could easily produce. Despite misleading talk of an affluent society, one American family out of eight is still earning less than $40 a week, and the average American still has only $38 a week to spend—a scant $4 increase in the last eight years.

Before discussing why a tax cut is advisable now—and what kind—we need discuss the broader problem of economic growth and stagnation.

Some would like to view this problem as involving a basic conflict between government and business. Nothing could be more absurd. Corporate profits after taxes declined an average of 11 per cent in the recession years of 1954 and 1958, and rose an average of 26 per cent in the recovery years of 1955 and 1959. Wages and salaries, by contrast, hardly declined in the recessions and rose less than 8 per cent in the recoveries. Business has a greater stake in growth than anyone else.

Unfortunately, business does not speak with a single voice on the importance of economic growth and profits. Many who claim to speak for business represent primarily the rentier interest, the owners of bonds and mortgages, who care little for the profitability of business in general but care a very great deal for price stability— or if possible, price declines—which would conserve or enhance the purchasing power of their fixed incomes or the value of their fixed-income securities. Many businessmen whose true interests lie in growth and profits have been taken in by the rentier propaganda emanating from banks, insurance companies, trust funds, realty groups, and "pro-business" journalists and politicians.

The stock market crash, which has hit particularly hard some of the so-called growth stocks, has also brought the validity of the growth goal into question. Yet the moment we think seriously about it, we must acknowledge that there is no real alternative. A growth company is simply one that is increasing its per share earnings rapidly and consistently. We cannot object to the fact that the market sets a higher value on the stocks of businesses that perform in such a manner. We can only object when they are overvalued even in relation to their rapid growth.

The stagnation in the earnings of so many of our blue-chip companies also accounts for many of the market's recent troubles. This stagnation is due partly to a shift in economic emphasis away from the older, more-or-less standardized industries, such as steel, textiles, railroads, automobiles, industrial machinery, etc., towards more modern research-intensive industries, such as plastics, drugs, missiles, electronics, instruments, etc. But it also reflects a general slowdown in industrial growth over the last eight years.

The last decade of American economic and business history breaks down into two sharply contrasting periods. From 1951 to 1953, during the Korean War, we had full employment (average unemployment of 3.1 per cent of the civilian labor force) and rapid industrial growth—averaging 7.2 per cent a year. From 1954 to 1961, by contrast, we have had a period of slow growth, with industrial output rising only about one third as fast as in the earlier period, with the average rate of unemployment around 75 per cent higher, and with a rising proportion of our industrial capacity lying unused. The average corporate profit after taxes in the dynamic earlier period was 5.3 per cent of Gross National Product, whereas the average since 1954 has been only 4.7 per cent—a percentage difference equal to $3.4 billions of profits at present levels of GNP.

To get back on the growth track we shall have to begin sensible Government budgeting on business-like principles—especially in the matter of the use of debt.

## Is Borrowing Immoral?

Progressive and growing businesses do not hesitate to draw upon outside credit resources when such resources can be effectively used and can contribute to sound (i.e., sustainable) expansion and profits, by making possible a sufficient expansion in production and sales, or reduction in unit costs. Bank credit is commonly utilized for financing of expansion in inventories, payrolls, exports, etc., and bonded indebtedness is accepted by sophisticated management for the purchase of new plant and equipment, when this can improve the profit "leverage" of invested equity capital. Corporations have been increasing their debts by $16.6 billion a year since 1953 —an amount sufficient to finance half of new investment in plant and equipment.

Modern businesses do not have emotional attitudes of fear or shame in thus utilizing debt. Debt is viewed not emotionally as an evil, but rationally as a convenience and a tool to be employed wherever, and up to the point, that it can make a useful contribution. Recognizing that the improvident use of credit may be a danger for weak characters, modern business presupposes that a sufficient degree of rationality and self-control for the wise use of debt-financing exists in responsible corporate officials. Particular debts must of course be repaid, but normally old debts are refinanced or new debts acquired, and while some businesses are always in the process of liquidating their debts, others are in the process of acquiring new debt.

This is just as well, since if all debts were suddenly paid off the economy would collapse. Our economy is largely based on debt formation. Our savings are not, on the whole, invested directly in productive enterprises. We do not, most of us, put our spare cash into the stock market. Instead, our personal savings are collected and invested by savings banks, pension funds, insurance companies, and so forth. These institutions are restrained by law and by custom from investing the bulk of our savings in common stock or other equities. Instead, they invest them largely in bank loans, mortgages and bonds. Somebody must therefore go into debt in order for somebody else's savings to be invested. The growth of the national income has therefore been pretty closely paralleled by the growth of debt—except during the Great Depression when the national income declined faster than debt could be liquidated. It is also relevant that the nation's money supply—which is itself closely related to the national income—is now largely a by-product of debt formation, since checking deposits (now comprising three quarters of the total money supply) are created mainly as the by-product of bank loans to businesses.

But while corporate debt financing is generally received as normal and entirely acceptable, Federal debt financing has been interpreted by the rentier groups as dangerous, improper and almost immoral—as, at best, a measure of expediency which may be unavoidable in emergencies or in recessions. Political capital has been made out of the size of the budget deficits, as if such deficits were necessarily discreditable; and a gullible public hearing these gibes endlessly repeated has assumed that there must be something in them.

There is one crucial difference in aims between government and business. Government is not—despite "Parkinson's law"—primarily in operation for its own benefit and growth, and is certainly not in operation to make a profit. Its basic purpose is to serve the welfare of the rest of the society—a purpose that can only be a secondary (though not necessarily a negligible) consideration for private business.

Because the effects of government taxing and spending are generally more important in what they do to the rest of the economy than in what they enable the government itself to do, they should be looked at primarily in terms of how they affect the private economy. How much purchasing power do taxes take away from private spenders (consumers and investors)? How many goods and services do government purchases divert from private to public use, and how much do they add to the income stream and to the total demand for private goods and services?

When there is much slack in the economy, increased government expenditures do not take *any* goods and services away from private users, but add to the income stream and to the demand for goods and services produced by private enterprises. Similarly, tax reductions at such a time increase the purchasing power available to private spenders (consumers and businesses) and raise activity in the private sector of the economy. The fact that such measures may involve "deficit financing" and "government borrowing" is not necessarily an argument against them. Just as private business may appropriately accept debt when this enables it to achieve profitable growth, so government may appropriately accept debt when this is the means for profitable growth—not its own growth, of course, but that of the private economy.

The rentier interest has consistently interpreted budget deficits as a sign of runaway spending. In reality, however, between 1953 and 1960 Federal per capita expenditures on goods and services, corrected for price increases, *declined* by 30 per cent. On a per capita basis, such expenditures—other than for defense—are now only half what they were back in 1939. The rise in government outlays since 1953 is attributable to a larger population, to the rising cost of goods and services, to increases in Social Security and other benefits made necessary by inflation, and to increased welfare spending because of spreading unemployment.

Exactly what is a Federal expenditure, receipt or deficit depends of course, on the definition used. The traditional "Administrative Budget" is not well suited to showing the true effects of the government's expenditures and receipts on the rest of the economy: it omits, for example, Social Security payroll taxes, and Social Security expenditures. It also grievously exaggerates the size of the deficits. . . . The traditional budget shows an average net deficit in the last eight years which is more than three times as high as is indicated by the more comprehensive and carefully designed budget of government outlays and receipts in the National Income and Product Account.

On the latter basis, it appears . . . that in half the years since 1953 the Federal Government has been taking away more purchasing power from private spenders (consumers and businesses) than it has been restoring to them by means of its own expenditures and benefit programs. The deficits that have nevertheless been encountered have arisen primarily as a result of a precipitate falloff in the tax base during recessions. Nine tenths of the total deficits since 1953 have been incurred in the three years of 1954, 1958 and 1961.

If there is one single factor which chiefly accounts for our slow growth since 1953, it is our high tax rates which prematurely

choked off our economic revivals by running up large budget surpluses (and curtailing private expenditure) in 1955-57, and 1960.
As William Butler, vice president of the Chase Manhattan Bank,
has shown, the rapid pace of private investment in 1955-57 would
not have led to excess capacity if only final demand had risen as
projected. The reason it couldn't . . . is that it was systematically
depleted by budget surpluses. With such surpluses, it will be
remembered, government takes away more private purchasing
power than it restores. There is *some* offsetting stimulus, to be
sure, when a budget surplus is used to retire public debt, since this
will, in the case of publicly held debt, raise bank reserves and facili-
tate bank loans. But this additional lending capacity is not really
the equivalent of the actual purchasing power destroyed by the
budget surplus, for the opportunity to borrow money that must be
repaid is not as expansionary as having the money and purchasing
power outright. The net effect of a surplus is therefore deflationary.

The attempt to achieve surpluses whenever possible has not
resulted in the avoidance of deficits; it has only assured that deficits
when they occurred would be of the "passive" variety—unwillingly
accepted, and imposed as a result of a declining or sluggish tax
base. With a greater willingness to court "active deficits," deliberately sought as a business stimulus, we might have ended with
a much more buoyant economy and with no larger a cumulative
deficit than we have now—indeed possibly with a smaller one.

The President understands this. He reminded reporters at his
August 1 [1962] press conference of the "1958 experience," when
there "was no tax cut and there was the largest peacetime deficit
in history because of a drop in income levels." However, he added,
the possibility of tax cuts this year must be considered not only
in light of further figures on the state of the economy which he
hopes to have by August 10, but also in the light of "the views of
the members of the House and Senate." In other words, Mr. Kennedy hesitates to start a fight in Congress with the large bloc which
still regards government borrowing to aid the economy as a concession to original sin. The President is also, it is said, being prodded by the Treasury to preserve the tax cut for use as a "sweetener"
next year to help win acceptance of the proposed tax reform bill.

*Prosperity Versus Reform*

Some of the tax reforms already proposed by the Treasury seem unsound to most business critics, including the writer; other proposed reforms may find more ready acceptance. But none of them, by the wildest stretch of imagination, could contribute anything like $30 to $40 billion a year to the national income—and that is what we are now losing by not being at full production. To hold up the immediate and urgent restoration of full national prosperity, in order to help put over a particular (and highly controversial) set of tax reforms, would illustrate to perfection the bureaucratic cast of mind and its sense of priorities.

But, as I have implied, the more basic difficulty is the implacable hostility in some congressional circles to government debt. Against the truly fundamentalist position on this issue it is futile to argue; we have to deal here with an irrational phobia rather than with a reasoned conviction. But where the opposition is rational to any degree, discussion is possible.

The notion, for example, that deficit financing leads to government extravagance and rising taxes, is clearly inapplicable when we are discussing deficit-financed tax cuts. Of course, revenues have to be raised to pay the interest charges on any increase in government debt, but the interest charge will be only a small percentage of the tax reduction, and the government may even recapture a large part of *that* by having the bonds sold to the Federal Reserve System, 90 per cent of the profits of which flow back to the government.

The public also assumes, despite recent contrary evidence, that deficit financing is necessarily dangerous for price stability. In fact, during the 1951 to 1953 period of heavy deficits and rapid growth, the price level (as measured by the broadest and truest gauge, the implicit Gross National Product deflators) rose only 1.5 per cent a year. On the other hand, during the 1953 to 1961 periods, where average net deficits were less than a third as large, prices rose on the average at 2 per cent a year. It is a striking fact that prices went up slightly more in the recession years of 1954 and 1958—when demand and production declined—than in the recovery years of 1955 and 1959, when demand and output were sharply up. All of which leads to the conclusion that a rise in output tends to be *disinflationary*, and that deficit financing, especially if it is used to expand production of consumer goods and services by utilizing unemployed manpower and industrial capacity, need not be inflationary at all. To be sure, the upward creep of costs will continue in any event, whether we have too much demand or too little, but this can't be helped by choking off production. It can be helped only by setting up self-imposed or externally imposed restraints on inflationary wage-price settlements.

Recently a new kind of objection to deficit financing has been gaining currency: it would undermine foreign confidence in the U.S. dollar and accentuate our balance of payment difficulties. Yet, as I tried to show in a recent book, *Europe at Sixes and Sevens: The Common Market, the Free Trade Association, and the United States*, the real situation may be almost the opposite. The slowdown in our growth rates and productivity gains, provoked by too restrictive fiscal policies, may have forced us into an increase in unit production costs, and may have thus weakened the international competitiveness of American manufacturers.

Europe, on the other hand, appears to owe its remarkable business progress in recent years (industrial output in the Common Market countries has increased four times as fast as in the United States since 1953) partly to more expansionist fiscal policies which have enabled its industries to achieve the overhead cost economies of full-capacity utilization.

Recent research suggests that if European and U.S. central government budgets are rearranged on a roughly comparable "cash" basis, the average deficit, from 1954 to 1959 inclusive, as a percentage of the Gross National Product appears as follows: United States 0.3 per cent, United Kingdom 0.6 per cent, West Germany 0.4 per cent, France 4.5 per cent. Thus, contrary to what is widely supposed, our European competitors have resorted, somewhat more freely than we have, to the use of deficit financing when necessary to stimulate their economies, and have avoided with more care than we the running of budgetary surpluses destructive of private purchasing power.

The Bank for International Settlements at Basle, which closely mirrors European bank sentiment, expressed the view in its last annual report that an increased use of deficit financing would benefit the U.S. economy and the position of the dollar, if accompanied by firm credit policies preserving high interest rates, thereby avoiding an outflow of short term capital from the United States in search of higher interest rates abroad. It is also remarkable that the United States Chamber of Commerce, which has been much concerned with the United States balance of payments and highly condemnatory of deficit financing in the past, has just repeated its call for a large tax cut, even at the expense of an increase in the budget deficit.

Still, if one assumes a tax cut is desirable, he is left with some difficult practical questions: How much? What type? How can it be done quickly? The questions are interrelated. . . .

[Consider for a moment a two-week "tax holiday"—that is, a two-week period in which no one paid income tax. This would, in effect, release 3.8 per cent of what is now collected in taxes back into the spending stream.] How would this work in practice and what would be its effects?

Let us assume that personal and corporate income taxes in calendar year 1962 will be around $70 billion. Three two-week tax holidays would then reduce these tax liabilities by $8 billion, roughly two thirds of which might be in personal taxes, and one third in corporate taxes. On the basis of the econometric model developed by Professor Suits at the University of Michigan (which has been highly successful in forecasting), it could be estimated that these tax cuts would raise the national output (GNP) by about possibly $8.3 billion, even assuming conservatively that corporate tax cuts have only half as dynamic an effect per dollar as personal tax cuts. Nearly 650,000 extra jobs would also be generated. The revenue loss to the Government would be not $8 billion, but only around $4.5 billion—since the tax cuts would stimulate a rise in income and tax yields.

But would the public actually spend as much of their tax savings as this estimate assumes? It is becoming fashionable in certain recherché circles to express a condescending skepticism about people's willingness to spend extra money if they had it. Reporters leap on the offhand comments of housewives, to the effect that if they had a few dollars extra a week they do not think they would buy anything "important" with it, but just fritter it away on day-to-day items. But $8 billion of small purchases are of economic importance too, like $8 billion of large purchases. Furthermore, the newly reemployed will certainly buy big-ticket items with their reestablished credit, and those benefiting from higher dividends and capital gains on their securities seem likely to buy luxuries. Obviously, the average housewife is not readily able to imagine the full ramifications of a sudden increase in income not only for her own family, but for all of her neighbors across the nation at the same time.

On a somewhat more scientific basis, it is worth noticing that the percentage of income after taxes spent by American consumers has remained extraordinarily stable, varying only between 92 and 94 per cent in every year since 1950, and never dropping below 91 per cent in any single quarter. A careful study of windfall additions to income through unexpected National Service Life Insurance dividends payments in 1950 found that unexpected extra income was spent in about the same proportions as other income. Other budget studies indicate that consumers normally spend two thirds of any *additional* income they receive within a year.

Such tax holidays would probably not, by themselves, restore full production and employment. They would, however, restore the economy's forward motion toward these goals, and give the Congress time enough to assess our long-term needs, to plug loopholes, and to consider the incentive and disincentive as well as the equity aspects of changing our tax patterns. They would also confer a tangible and easy-to-understand benefit on virtually every breadwinner and every business, and would, I am willing to wager, be extraordinarily popular with the electorate and hence not entirely devoid of appeal to the Congress this year.

# III.  TAXES TAKE THE LIMELIGHT

## EDITOR'S INTRODUCTION

Once it became clear in the early 1960's that the U.S. economy *should* grow faster, that fiscal policy (and specifically, reduction of the tax load) was the best tool to accomplish just that, the spotlight of national attention fell on taxes.

This section focuses on taxation in general and on Federal Government taxing in particular. The first article, by tax scholar E. R. A. Seligman, is a history of how taxes came about and why men paid them. Even more interesting, it traces how the popular concept of taxation gradually changed from one of contribution to one of obligation.

The next three selections deal with Federal taxation. The Federal Government has two main sources of income—excise taxes and income taxes. As the Government's largest sources of income—and because they affect almost everyone in the nation—they also become the Government's main tax tools in economic policy.

The first of these three articles charts the growth of excise taxes in the United States; these are taxes on the manufacture, sale, or use of commodities. The next selection deals with a relatively short-lived income tax imposed during the Civil War. After that conflict ended income taxes gradually faded and it was not until the early 1900's that Congress again became interested in this source of income. Then in 1913 the Congress passed the one-paragraph Sixteenth Amendment, which gave it the legal right to tax incomes, and the income tax has been an institution ever since. The last of this group of articles traces the growth of income taxes since the Sixteenth Amendment to 1962.

The last article in the section, written by a *Wall Street Journal* staff reporter, relates directly to using taxes to stimulate the economy. Having grown to mammoth proportions, Federal income taxes were on the cutting block in 1964. The article describes the specific hopes the Administration had for increases in employment and a heightened pace of business activity as a result of the $11.5 billion slash.

## THE DEVELOPMENT OF TAXATION [1]

To the citizen of the modern state, taxation, however disagreeable it may be, seems natural. It is difficult to realize that it is essentially a recent growth and that it marks a comparatively late stage in the development of public revenue; it is more difficult to realize that each age has its own system of public revenue, and that the taxes of today are different from those of former times; it is still more difficult to perceive that our ideals of justice in taxation change with the alteration in social conditions. Not only the actual forms of taxation, but the theories of taxation as well, vary with the economic basis of society. Fiscal conditions are always an outcome of economic relations. This is true even where the direct influence of political causes is traceable, for political changes are in the last resort dependent on economic changes. Finance and economics are inextricably intertwined. Like all the facts of social life, taxation itself is only an historical category.

At the beginning of history there is no such thing as a state. Whether we accept Hobbes' theory of the *bellum omnium contra omnes* [war of each against all] or the more modern clan theory of the origin of society, there is no public household, because there are no recognized public needs. But even in the original man there are possibilities of social development. Man, as Aristotle tells us, is a social and political animal. Centuries of hard experience strengthen the social instinct and contribute to form primitive society, until finally a real political life emerges.

Gradually from either physical, ethical or religious causes a leader evolves. The oldest or the wisest or the bravest—at all events, the one possessed of some peculiar characteristic—becomes the leader of the horde, the clan or the tribe. He acts as the great priest, great judge or great warrior, often combining all three qualities. There are no financial needs, because the only consideration

[1] From *Essays in Taxation,* by Edwin R. A. Seligman. Macmillan. New York. '25. p 1-5. Reprinted by permission. The late author was McVickar Professor of Political Economy at Columbia University and an authority on taxation.

is that of defense; and every man contributes to the defense in his own person. The leader himself subsists on the booty of war.

But with the growth of society and the expansion of the clan into the larger community, the public needs develop. Administration begins. Roads, bridges and fortifications are constructed, and the prince or king must now not only maintain order, but must be assured of a revenue to support his household and to distribute favors to his retinue. All his followers, being roughly equal, now support him by gifts, whether of labor or of property. In all primitive societies voluntary offerings constitute the first form of common contributions, and every man feels the necessity of upholding the political and military organization by his own personal efforts.

The king's needs now increase. They are chiefly personal needs, except in so far as expenditures are made for the purposes of internal peace and external defense. But in order to ensure his position, the king endeavors to secure his revenues elsewhere. He develops the subsidies and tributes of the allied and conquered nations, and amasses treasure filched from abroad. Part of this he distributes among his followers; part he retains to increase his own possessions. The private property of the king differentiates itself from the public property, which was originally common to all. The monarch now increases his revenues and domains through the acquisition of lucrative prerogatives of all kinds. Certain activities come to be looked upon as within his peculiar province. The king's peace must be kept—any infraction must be paid for in fines and penalties; not only crimes, but torts, have their public side. Nobody can harm an individual without breaking the king's peace, and having to pay for it. Commerce begins, and weights and measures and money are needed. The royal rights of coinage arise; and as the kingship becomes stronger, the rights of escheat, of wreck, of confiscation develop, until finally the various royal prerogatives bring in a substantial revenue.

Voluntary payments have in the meantime ceased. As society advances, what was at the outset freely given comes to be paid by the individual from a sense of moral obligation. But with the weakness of human nature, in the face of a diversity of interests, even the feeling of duty soon fails to produce an adequate revenue.

The moral obligation slowly becomes a legal obligation, keeping pace with the crystallization of social usage and custom into primitive law; the voluntary offerings become compulsory contributions. But the compulsory contributions are still largely personal services, connected with the common security. Such was the early medieval *trinoda necessitas,* the liability to military service, to watch and ward, and to the repair of the bridges and fortifications. The first forced contribution of the individual to the maintenance of the common welfare is always seen in this rude attempt to assess every one according to his ability to bear the common burden—his faculty. This faculty consists in the enforced participation in the administration. But there is not yet any idea of taxation of property. The contribution is personal, and is limited to a few well-defined objects. The individual's faculty is found in his person, not in his property, because there is practically no private property. And the contributions are, for the most part, not regular, but spasmodic.

As civilization gradually advances, private property develops, and the primitive equality slowly disappears. The interchange of commodities takes place on a larger scale. The old revenues are no longer adequate, and it becomes necessary for the monarch to supplement them by broadening the field of these compulsory contributions of service. In other words, the need of taxation arises. But a direct tax is still out of the question. Public opinion will not yet admit its necessity. The taxation of property is scarcely less impossible than the taxation of the person. It is regarded as a badge of disgrace for the freeman—a *nota captivitatis,* as the Romans at first called it—because only conquered enemies have to pay this arbitrary impost. The king, therefore, must endeavor to effect his object covertly. He must go to work in a roundabout way, and hide the tax in a variety of disguises. He either gradually extends his lucrative prerogatives, or alleges that the charges are simple returns for governmental services. He grants protection or privileges to individuals, and requires some payment in return. Thus begins the period of fees and charges, which the individuals are willing to pay and which gradually reconcile the public to the idea of governmental charges.

Before long, however, the monarch feels able to throw off all disguises, and limits the amount of his exactions only by the degree of his rapacity. Thus the fees and tolls change into taxes on exchange and transportation; thus the people become accustomed to the "customs"; thus the "evil duties" and the excises grow apace; thus the payments become veritable "impositions." In other words, the community enters upon the stage of indirect taxation.

This explains why it is so difficult for the idea of direct taxation to force its way into popular favor. The earliest manifestations of the taxing power are generally merciless and brutal. They are apt to react on the public consciousness and to stunt the growth of any feeling of obligation. It is not until public morality has so far developed as to introduce more lenient and more refined processes of indirect taxation that we discover a growing willingness on the part of the individual to pay direct taxes. Another reason for the later appearance of direct taxation is that the indirect taxes are often paid without the contributors being really conscious of it. They are jealous of their own and not public-spirited. They are willing to give only that the loss of which they do not feel. But whatever be the reason, it is clear that when this final stage—possible only after centuries of laborious and continued exertion—has been reached, we enter upon a new phase in the history of finance. The readiness to share in the public burdens out of one's property presupposes a far higher social ethics and a far more complex society than was possible in the simple conditions when everyone was willing to take part in the defense of the village or the repair of the roads. Interests have now become specialized. It needs a far greater sense of civic obligation to submit cheerfully to direct property taxation than was necessary in primitive times for the putting forth of mere personal exertions. Even today the full import of this obligation is only inadequately grasped. Until within a few years it was deemed necessary to base the theoretical justification of taxation on fanciful doctrines of contract, of protection and the like. And even at the present time, those who cheerfully seek to contribute their share to the common burden form the exception, not the rule. But even the imperfect recognition of this duty implies a highly developed political consciousness. The method of taxing everyone according to his property is the first rough attempt of a property-owning community (as over against a primitive community) to assess each member according to his relative ability. The introduction of the direct property tax is a vast step forward in the development of social ethics.

This historical process is well illustrated by etymology. If we look at the various terms applied to what we today call a tax, we shall find every shade of the development reflected not only in the words used in former centuries, but in those still employed today. There are no less than seven different stages in this etymological growth.

The original idea was that of gift. The individual made a present to the government. We see this in the medieval Latin term *donum* and in the English *benevolence,* which was used far into the middle ages. The second stage was reached when the government humbly implored or prayed the people for support. This is the meaning of the Latin *precarium,* used for many centuries on the continent, as well as of the German *Bede* (from *beten,* to pray). The *Landbede* was the term applied to the land tax in the German states until quite recently. With the third stage we come to the idea of assistance to the state. The individual felt that, if not making a gift, he was at least doing the government a favor. This idea is expressed in the Latin *adjutorium,* the English *aid* and the French *aide,* which was at one time used for all kinds of taxes. The same idea is discernible in the English *subsidy* and *contribution.* It has survived in the German term for a tax, *Steuer* (*steuern,* to help), and in the Scandinavian *hjelp.* In France *contribution* is even today commonly used as synonymous with tax.

The fourth stage of development brings out the idea of sacrifice by the individual in the interest of the state. He now surrenders something for the public good. This is seen in the old French *gabelle,* in the modern German *Abgabe,* and in the familiar Italian *dazio.* In each case the citizen gives or sacrifices something. With the fifth stage the feeling of obligation develops in the taxpayer. The English *duty* was not originally restricted to its present narrow meaning in the United States. Here it is usually applied to import taxes and sometimes to the internal revenue taxes. But even today in England the term includes some of the most important so-called direct taxes, like the inheritance tax and the income tax. It is not until the sixth stage is reached that we meet the idea of compulsion on the part of the state. We see this in our *impost* or *imposition,* as well as in the French *impôt* and the Italian *imposta.* Although we limit the term to a certain kind of tax, the French use it as the generic epithet *par excellence.* The same idea is seen in the German *Auflage* (something "laid on") and *Aufschlag* (something "clapped on"), frequently used at present for certain indirect charges on commodities.

With the seventh and final stage we reach the idea of a rate or assessment, fixed or estimated by the government without any reference to the volition of the taxpayer. We see this in the medieval English *scot* (to be "at scot and lot"), which is nothing but the German *Schoss* or the Scandinavian *skatt.* It is seen in the German *Schätzung* (or estimate), which was used until about a century ago. Above all, it is recognized in our *tax* (*taxare,* to fix, to estimate), the French *taxe,* the Italian *tassa* and the English *rate.* It is worthy of note that in the middle ages "tax" always meant a direct tax, for which a regular assessment list or schedule was made.

## EXCISE TAXES [2]

Almost all excises now in force were imposed originally as war taxes. At their inception, such levies were generally regarded as temporary sources of revenue which would not be needed when conditions returned to normal. Most excises, however, have outlived the emergencies that brought them into being. Liquor taxes were collected from 1791 to 1802 to meet charges on the public debt, and from 1812 to 1817 to help finance the War of 1812. They were reintroduced in 1862, second year of the Civil War, and have remained on the statute books ever since.

Taxes on admissions and club dues and on narcotics, and certain stamp taxes, date from World War I years. The only excise introduced in time of peace, collected for more than fifty years and still in effect, is the stamp tax on playing cards, first imposed in

[2] From "Excise Tax Cuts and the Economy," by Richard L. Worsnop, staff writer. *Editorial Research Reports.* 1, no 11:208-14. Mr. 24, '65. Reprinted by permission.

1894. All of the foregoing imposts—on liquor, tobacco, admissions, narcotics, and playing cards—have been collected for so long a time that they are commonly regarded as permanent parts of the Federal tax system.

Virtually the only excises in effect in the United States when war broke out in Europe in 1914 were tobacco, alcoholic beverage and stamp taxes. The annual yield of these levies was about $300 million. American entry into the war in 1917 brought imposition of a host of new excises, including manufacturers' taxes on various products, admissions taxes, and imposts on telephone, telegraph and cable messages. Federal excise tax collections reached a peak of $901 million in fiscal 1920, despite the fact that liquor tax revenue had fallen drastically because of prohibition.

Repeal and reduction of the World War I excises began three years after the Armistice of 1918, but nearly a decade went by before the last of the emergency levies was removed. Taxes on transportation of passengers and freight, and excises on such products as sporting goods and cosmetics, furs and umbrellas, chewing gum and vacuum bottles, were lifted on January 1, 1922, by an act which also cut the rates of some of the remaining nuisance taxes. In mid-1924 levies on telephone and telegraph messages, on candy and soft drinks, and on rugs, luggage and other items were repealed. The Revenue Act of 1926 wiped the slate almost clean, removing excises on cameras, jewelry, watches, clocks, automobile trucks, tires, parts and accessories, and a few additional articles. But the wartime tax on sales of passenger automobiles and motorcycles, reduced in 1926, survived until its repeal in 1928. Excise tax collections in fiscal 1930 totaled only $565 million, of which $450 million came from levies on tobacco products.

### Proliferation of Excise Taxes in the Depression

The Federal Government was forced to reintroduce many of the repealed wartime excises in 1932 to compensate for a drastic decline in receipts from income taxes. Individual and corporate income taxes yielded only $747 million in fiscal 1933, or about one third as much as they had three years earlier. Accordingly, the Revenue

Act of 1932 increased admissions and stamp taxes and imposed more than a score of manufacturers' and miscellaneous imposts.

The new levies included taxes on passenger cars, trucks, automobile parts and accessories; gasoline and lubricating oil; telegrams and long-distance telephone calls; toilet preparations, furs, jewelry, sporting goods and cameras; radios, phonographs, records and mechanical refrigerators. Repeal of the prohibition amendment in 1933 again made the liquor excise an important source of revenue. Thus, while income tax revenue did not reach predepression levels until 1938, excise tax collections increased sharply. Excise tax revenue in fiscal 1934 came to $1.3 billion, four times the amount that had been collected in fiscal 1932. In the four fiscal years from 1933 to 1936, excise taxes produced more revenue than did income taxes.

Excise taxes imposed by the Revenue Act of 1932 were scheduled to expire automatically in the summer of 1934, but most of them were extended to 1935 and then successively renewed, at the same rates, for two-year periods. The levies on candy, soft drinks, bank checks, and use of pleasure boats were repealed in 1935; the tax on jewelry in 1936; and the excises on chewing gum, furs, phonograph records, cameras and sporting goods in 1938. But the Revenue Act of 1940, which became law shortly after the fall of France, extended the remaining 1932 excise taxes, then due to expire in 1941, for a four-year period to end in 1945. The same act established higher "defense tax rates," to continue until 1945, for most of the surviving 1932 excises, for liquor and cigarette taxes, and for certain miscellaneous taxes.

### Rate Increases and New Levies in World War II

The continued 1932 excises were made permanent by the Revenue Act of 1941, as were some of the defense tax rates; other defense tax rates and various other rates were approximately doubled, while numerous new excises were imposed. Jewelry, furs, sporting goods, and other articles were again taxed, and excises were imposed on such previously untaxed products as electric light bulbs, luggage, photographic equipment, and business machines. The 1941 Act also imposed an automobile use tax and a 5 per cent tax on transportation of persons by train, bus, ship or plane. The Revenue Act of 1942 raised the passenger transportation tax to 10 per cent, levied a 3 per cent tax on transportation of property by rail, motor vehicle, water or air, and increased the rates of communications, liquor, tobacco and a number of other excises.

World War II excise taxation reached its peak in 1944 with application of the so-called war tax rates on communications and transportation of persons; on jewelry, furs, toilet preparations, and electric light bulbs; on liquor, beer and wine; and on admissions and club dues. These rate increases helped to boost excise tax revenue from $4.5 billion in fiscal 1944 to $5.9 billion in fiscal 1945— a net gain of $1.4 billion.

### Imposition and Extension of Korean War Excises

By 1950, annual excise tax collections had leveled off at around $7.5 billion. The revenue act of that year started out as a measure to slash excises by about $1 billion, the loss to be made up largely by higher corporate income tax rates. Outbreak of the Korean War in June 1950 forced a change of approach. Existing excise tax rates were extended, and two new taxes were added—10 per cent manufacturers' levies on television sets and freezing units.

Confronted by soaring defense costs, Congress in 1951 approved legislation to increase tax revenue by $5.7 billion, of which $1.2 billion was to come from new and higher excise rates. Among the new taxes were a 10 per cent levy on wagers placed with bookmakers and lottery operators, and a $50 annual occupational tax on persons accepting such wagers. These two taxes were criticized as lending an aura of respectability to activities that were illegal in most states.

The Revenue Act of 1951 imposed 15 per cent manufacturers' levies on cigar, cigarette and pipe lighters and on fountain pens, ballpoint pens and mechanical pencils. The existing 10 per cent tax on electric, gas and oil appliances was applied to a number of previously exempt products, including belt-driven fans, clothes driers, door chimes, dehumidifiers, dishwashers, floor polishers and waxers, hedge trimmers, and other items. Diesel fuel was subjected to a 2 cents-per-gallon levy.

Most of the excise revision in 1951 involved increases of existing rates. The cigarette tax was raised from 7 cents to 8 cents a pack, while wine and liquor taxes were raised by various amounts. The impost on beer went up from $8 to $9 a barrel. Increases in manufacturers' excises fell exclusively on automotive products. The prevailing 7 per cent rate on passenger cars, automobile trailers and motorcycles was boosted to 10 per cent, while the 5 per cent levy on trucks, trailers, road tractors, parts and accessories mounted to 8 per cent. Gasoline, taxed at 1.5 cents a gallon since 1940, was subjected to a 2 cents-a-gallon levy.

The Revenue Act of 1951 provided that all excise rate increases were to expire automatically on March 31, 1954. As it turned out, none of them did; the Excise Reduction Act of 1954 extended all of the 1951 rate increases for one year. However, the 1954 Act slashed a number of other rates, some of which had been in effect since World War II. It reduced to 10 per cent the former 20 per cent tax on furs, jewelry, luggage, toilet preparations, electric light bulbs and tubes, cameras, lenses and film, safe deposit box rental, and most general admissions. The 25 per cent tax on long distance telephone calls and the 15 per cent tax on sporting goods, mechanical pens, pencils and lighters, transportation and local telephone and telegraph messages were also cut to 10 per cent.

The Federal excise tax structure has undergone almost no basic change in the past decade. The emergency rate increases of 1951, extended in 1954, have been reextended for one-year periods in every subsequent session of Congress. The 3 per cent levy on transportation of property was repealed in 1958, and the taxes on general telephone service and on transportation of persons by railroad, bus, plane and water, originally imposed in 1941, were made subject to annual extensions in 1959. The following year, annual extension of excise taxes met strong but unavailing opposition in the Senate. Efforts made in both Senate and House in 1961 to repeal the passenger transportation taxes were unsuccessful. In 1962, however, the levies on travel by railroad, bus and water were repealed and the tax on air travel was cut from 10 to 5 per cent. The only new excise of any consequence introduced in the past decade is the levy imposed in 1956 on highway vehicles weighing more than 26,000 pounds.

## *Excise Tax Receipts—Yield of Particular Taxes*

The excise tax reductions approved in 1954 resulted in a $300 million drop in excise revenue in fiscal 1955. Since then, excise tax collections have increased every year except one; in the past three fiscal years, the annual increase has averaged about $650 million. If the rates in force today were to remain in effect for another year, excise tax revenue almost certainly would exceed $15 billion for the first time.

There are at present almost 150 different excise taxes, listed under six general headings by the Treasury Department—liquor, tobacco, stamp, manufacturers' excise, retailers' excise, and miscellaneous. The most productive of these categories is that including the various manufacturers' excises, which together will yield about $6.2 billion in fiscal 1965. About five sixths of that amount, or $5.2 billion, will come from levies on gasoline, passenger cars, trucks, buses and tractors, and tires and inner tubes. The least productive type of excise is the stamp tax, levied on issuance and transfers of stocks and bonds, conveyances of documents, foreign insurance policies, and playing cards.

Among the individual excises, that on gasoline is the most important; gasoline tax revenue is expected to total $2.7 billion in the current fiscal year. The next three most lucrative sources of excise revenue are the taxes on distilled spirits ($2.6 billion in fiscal 1965), on cigarettes ($2.1 billion) and on passenger cars and motorcycles ($1.8 billion). No other individual excise yields as much as $1 billion a year.

Among the retailers' excises, . . . the taxes on jewelry and on toilet preparations each produce about $200 million a year. By contrast, the levies on luggage, handbags and wallets, and on furs and fur articles, yield only $82 million and $31 million a year, respectively. Annual revenue from the tax on diesel fuel, committed to the Highway Trust Fund until 1972, is about $140 million.

Many excises are of only marginal value from a revenue standpoint. The tax on matches, for example, will produce an estimated $4 million in fiscal 1965—some $1.8 million less than a decade earlier. The snuff tax yield is so small that it has been lumped together with chewing and smoking tobacco revenue since fiscal 1959. Other excises that will produce less than $15 million in fiscal 1965 include those on mechanical pens, pencils and lighters ($10 million), safe-deposit box rental ($8 million) and bowling alleys and billiard and pool tables ($6 million). The controversial wagering excise brings in only $7 million a year—a mere fraction of the amount that would be collected if every bettor and bookie complied with revenue laws.

[As the need for revenues became acute after 1965, the Federal Government postponed some of the scheduled cuts. See note at end of "The Second Cut, 1965" in Section I, above.—Ed.]

## UNITED STATES INCOME TAX—1862-1913 [3]

The income tax, the nation's most affluent fount of revenue and the most ingenious instrument ever devised to bring about the redistribution of wealth, was initiated one hundred years ago. In July 1862, President Lincoln signed the first income-tax law ever put in operation by the Federal Government.

Almost every sort of tax had been tried out by Secretary of the Treasury Alexander Hamilton and his successors in office. And, although Alexander J. Dallas, Treasury Secretary during the War of 1812, proposed an income tax, the Government managed to balance its budget, meet its deficits and fund its debts for some seventy-three years before being forced to adopt that desperate expedient.

If times of crisis embolden statesmen to create new instruments to attain their ends, the summer of 1862 was such a time. The discouraging Peninsular Campaign had brought the war no closer to an end. Ever since the first Battle of Bull Run the North had suffered setbacks and military frustrations. It was now clear to all who cared to see that the war would be long and it would be costly. The North's purse, however, was empty.

"The expenditures everywhere are frightful," Secretary of the Treasury Salmon P. Chase wrote in the fall of 1861. The former

[3] From "100 Years of Income Outgo," by Richard B. Morris, member of the Department of History, Columbia University. New York *Times Magazine.* p 55. Ag. 5, '62. © 1962 by The New York Times Company. Reprinted by permission.

Senator from Ohio, a man consumed with ambition for the presidency, had many capabilities, but they did not lie along financial lines. His ideas about revenue were pretty conventional. He counted heavily on the tariff for the bulk of Federal income.

But with the coming of the Civil War imports fell off drastically, accompanied by an alarming drop in customs revenue. Something else had to be tried, and before the income tax was resorted to Chase attempted with considerable difficulty to sell Government bonds. In addition Treasury notes were issued, and the Morill Tariff of 1861 was supplemented by an extensive list of excise taxes, so comprehensive that it took thirty pages to list them.

Men ruefully recalled Sydney Smith's outcry over the taxes imposed by Britain to resist Napoleon:

> Taxes on everything which it is pleasant to see, hear, feel, smell, or taste; taxes . . . on the sauce which pampers man's appetite and on the drug that restores him to health; on the ermine which decorates the judge and the rope which hangs the criminal; on the poor man's sauce and the rich man's spice; on the brass nails of the coffin and the ribbons of the bride.

Also in 1861, Congress enacted an income tax of 3 per cent on all incomes over $800 a year, but this was never put into effect largely because Secretary Chase persuaded Congress to try less severe means first. However, even Chase soon saw that the time was past for timid steps. Bold remedies were called for, and in 1862 Congress provided a cluster of them, including a new income tax, which this time was put into effect.

The Internal Revenue Act of 1862 embodied the basic features of our present income tax: individual tax returns, graduated rates, minimum exemptions and even salary withholding. The tax amounted to 3 per cent on incomes below $10,000, 5 per cent above that figure, with a personal exemption of $600. It even covered the American citizen resident abroad, who was obliged to pay 5 per cent on all income derived from the United States.

The 1862 measure allowed deductions for "all other national, state, and local taxes." Following the practice Great Britain inaugurated in 1803, the law provided that the 3 per cent tax be withheld from the salaries of all persons in the civil, military or naval service of the United States.

The withholding principle went a step further, anticipating proposals . . . recommended by the Kennedy Administration. It extended withholding to interest or dividends paid on railroad bonds or stocks, and on all dividends paid by banks, trust companies, savings institutions and insurance firms. Such withholding of dividends and interest at the source was then considered perfectly equitable and practical, and it does not seem to have occurred to the banks or insurance companies that the procedure was "bad," "unfair" and "unworkable," to choose among the milder epithets used today.

It would not be correct to assume that the leveling features of the income tax of 1862 escaped unnoticed. Senator Thaddeus Stevens, who normally relished radical causes, denounced the progressive income tax rates as "a punishment of the rich man because he is rich," and Representative Justin S. Morrill, sponsor of the high protective tariff which bore his name, excoriated it as "no less than a confiscation of property, because one man happens to have a little more money than another," and held it up as evidence of "the spirit of agrarianism," a label which in the 1860's was as derogatory as "communism" is today.

Still, the tax rates were stepped up in 1864 and again in 1865. The public found no cause for alarm when A. T. Stewart, the New York department store magnate, paid one check of $400,000 on an income of $4 million. "Every man's property, and every man's income, should be, and, we trust, will be taxed," said the New York *Times*, expressing a widely prevalent view.

Once the Civil War began to fade into memory the public was unwilling to bear these tax burdens any longer. Rates were halved in 1870. Then a fiscal surplus, combined with mounting criticism from business interests, brought about the repeal of the income tax in 1872. During the decade it was on the books it had brought in an estimated revenue of $370 million.

In terms of later constitutional history it is significant that in the debates over the Civil War income tax its sponsors took its constitutionality for granted, and nobody seriously contested it on those grounds at the time. When, in 1894, the income tax was re-instituted as a result of Populist pressures, its constitutionality was challenged in the courts, and the Supreme Court invalidated it. It was not until the eve of World War I that Congress' power to levy an income tax was clarified by the Sixteenth Amendment.

[The text of the Sixteenth Amendment reads: "The Congress shall have power to lay and collect taxes on incomes, from whatever source derived, without apportionment among the several States, and without regard to any census or enumeration."—Ed.]

Enacted in response to the military and fiscal crisis of 1862, the Federal income tax marked a revolution in the American way of life. Its use for a decade and then its revival in the twentieth century brought home the burdens of government to each and every individual in the country and tore down many of the comfortable tax shelters in which privileged groups had been able for so long to hide, shifting to others the costs of government.

The huge gusher of tax revenue which the Federal Government had struck enabled it to enlarge enormously the scope of its operations. As demands upon it burgeoned with the years its appetite became increasingly voracious. That appetite is not yet sated, nor have the calls become less insistent upon the Federal Treasury from all corners of the globe, not to speak of outer space.

## UNITED STATES INCOME TAX SINCE 1913 [4]

The Federal income tax next year [1963] will celebrate its golden jubilee—the fiftieth anniversary of the Sixteenth Amendment to the United States Constitution. Right now it looks more like a year of stormy debate than a year of celebration for a tax that has never been popular yet, paradoxically, was woven into the Constitution by popular demand.

An unusually determined and bipartisan reform movement, backed by many nonpolitical economists, is being built up in growing discontent with the economic effects of the tax system as it stands.

[4] Article, "The Income Tax and How It Grew." *Business Week*. p 128-30. Je. 23, '62. Reprinted from the June 23, 1962 issue of *Business Week* by special permission. Copyrighted © 1962 by McGraw-Hill, Inc.

President Kennedy said this month [June 1962] that he will seek across-the-board tax cuts in 1963, and the Republican party next day officially called for a thorough overhaul of the tax system. [After various delays tax cuts were finally made in 1964 and 1965. See "The First Tax Cut, 1964" and "The Second Cut, 1965" in Section I, above.—Ed.] The purposes of the income tax are being reevaluated, along with questions of how well the present tax structure is serving these purposes.

### Triple Purpose

In its two previous brief and not very effective incarnations and in its career since 1913, the Federal income tax system supposedly aims at three objectives. These have been clouded as superstructure was built on structure, but originally they were:

### To pay for wars

The first Federal income tax was passed during the Civil War; later it was abolished. After being reinstituted in 1913, it was sharply increased during World War I; afterward, it was cut back equally sharply. It first became an instrument of mass taxation during the unprecedentedly costly World War II, and after the fighting ended it remained the Government's biggest revenue producer. The United States continued to fight a new kind of war, the cold war in which the free world looked to the United States for leadership.

### To redistribute income

The affirmation of the right of the Federal Government to levy an income tax, through the Sixteenth Amendment, was the result of twenty-five years of agitation by Populists and muckrakers against, as one of their attorneys put it, "the growing concentration of wealth in an ever-diminishing number of persons." The present pyramiding of rates is traceable to Franklin D. Roosevelt's drive in the 1930's to curb the power and wealth of what he called "the economic royalists."

*To curb inflation*

When World War II broke out, Congress was determined to avert another serious inflation like that of World War I. It levied stiff taxes on the broad mass of taxpayers. The stated purpose of Beardsley Ruml's "pay as you go" withholding plan was "to convert the income tax into a flexible instrument for the control of inflation."

### Civil War Era

The first Federal income tax, imposed in 1861, was at a flat rate of 3 per cent on incomes above $800. As the war went on, the rate was increased, ultimately to a top of 15 per cent on incomes above $15,000. Despite poor enforcement and widespread evasion, the tax yielded substantial revenues.

Between the Civil War and World War I came an era of fast economic growth and small government. So there was little or no pressure for income taxes to raise revenue; most of the money the Federal Government needed came from customs duties. The unpopular Civil War income tax was lowered in 1867 and abolished in 1872.

### Age of Reformers

The next chapter in the history of the income tax was not the story of a government in search of revenues but of social reformers in search of a means of curbing the great concentrations of wealth in the nation's rapid industrialization.

Through agitation of Populist farmers in the West who were determined to curb the financial power of Eastern bankers and industrialists, a new income tax law was put through Congress in 1894. But this act was invalidated by the Supreme Court. The reform drive didn't fully succeed until 1913, when Wyoming became the thirty-sixth state to ratify the Sixteenth Amendment.

### Another War

The tax law's aim of redistributing wealth wasn't destined to remain dominant, for World War I began before the tax system developed far. The tax's first big job became that of financing the war.

In 1918, the Federal income tax—still mild by present standards—extended from 6 per cent on the first $4,000 of income to 77 per cent on $1 million or more. Economists have been arguing for years that the rapid inflation of World War I came at least partly from congressional reluctance to impose high rates on the mass of consumers.

As was the case after the Civil War, the 1920's became a period of tax reduction. President Calvin Coolidge led the drive to cut taxes. "If we are to adopt socialism," he said, "it should be presented to the people of the country as socialism and not under the guise of a law to collect revenue."

A series of tax cuts brought the bottom-bracket rate down to ⅜ per cent by 1929, the top-bracket rate down to 24 per cent.

### New Deal, New War

The New Deal revived the old Populist arguments and put teeth in them. Tax legislation of 1936 and 1937 boosted the personal income rates in the upper brackets and, more significantly, bit more deeply into corporate income. By 1939, Roosevelt had put the top personal tax rate, which had been 63 per cent when he took office in 1933, up to 79 per cent. But the rate on the first $4,000 was still only 4 per cent.

It took World War II to turn what had been essentially a tax on the classes into a tax on the masses. By the end of the war, the rate on the bottom bracket reached 23 per cent and the top rate reached 94 per cent. By then, 50 million taxpayers—38 per cent of the population—were filing returns, compared with 6 million in 1937.

The crowning touch was Ruml's withholding plan, collecting the bulk of personal income taxes at the source. This plan has made the income tax the potent system it is for collecting revenue from the mass of taxpayers. It makes mass income taxation administratively feasible by keeping improvident taxpayers from becoming tax evaders by spending their tax accruals before the day of reckoning.

### Economic Device

The combination of high rates and tax withholding also proved during World War II to be a powerful economic device. It greatly helped the Office of Price Administration in controlling inflation during the war, and it is regarded as an important reason that no "hyperinflation" followed the removal of price controls after V-J Day.

Today's question is whether this tax structure, basically the same as it was during World War II, is still timely. Many economists see it as still trying to do the wartime job of preventing hyperinflation in a new period when this condition is no longer a threat.

These economists say the present tax structure is throwing the national economy out of gear. With backlogs of consumer demand already filled and with an excess of capacity holding back investment demand, the tax system carried over from years of war and boom is still trying to force the economy to save as if a war or a capital spending boom were still raging.

As more and more economists and Government officials recognize this condition as a drag on the economy, the big question in the coming year will be what tax burdens should be cut in order to open the way for renewed growth.

## ACTION AND REACTION [5]

In arguing for the tax cut, Administration officials didn't rely only on the contention that it would aid the economy as a whole; they also showed detailed estimates of how it would benefit each segment. These estimates may be somewhat awry by now, however, because Congress missed the January 1 [1964] target date for passing the bill.

To make up for the delay, Congress accepted President Johnson's suggestion that the rate at which taxes are withheld from paychecks be cut to 14 per cent from the present 18 per cent, in one immediate step instead of two. This adds to the extra money available at once to consumers, but there are no plans for immediately revising the estimated economic benefits. Authorities . . . , in saying this, add a

[5] From "Waiting for the Boom," article by Richard Janssen, staff reporter. *Wall Street Journal.* p 3+. F. 27, '64. Reprinted by permission.

thought rarely expressed during the Capitol Hill battle: that economic forecasting is, after all, an inexact science.

President Johnson did allow for some lag in enactment when he forecast in his January Economic Message that the gross national product would rise to about $623 billion this year from $585 billion last year if passage came by February 1. But if the bill were delayed until March 1, he said, the GNP target would be $621 billion. The GNP is a measure of the total market value of the output of U.S. goods and services; as usual with the year-ahead forecast, the target is understood to be the midpoint of a $10 billion range.

Official forecasts of what would happen to the economy without the tax cut all have been on the dire side. If taxes weren't pared this year, the President has predicted, GNP would be $10 billion to $15 billion less than last year's and "dashed expectations" might well tumble the nation into a recession. A recession no worse than those in 1957-58 and 1960-61, he said, would drop GNP by $25 billion a year, add about 2 million people to the 4.5 million currently unemployed, and slash about $5 billion from the present $27.5 billion annual rate of corporate after-tax profits.

The forecasts of greater prosperity rely much on the assumption that Americans will continue spending about 93 cents of each dollar of after-tax income. The tax cut reduces individuals' tax bills this year [1964] by some $6.1 billion; the figure grows to $9.1 billion next year.

Authorities appear certain that most of this money will be spent rather than saved, reasoning that more than half goes to those with annual incomes of $10,000 or less; usually, the lower on the income scale, the greater proportion spent, they say. With a new minimum standard deduction, some 1.5 million low-income families may be spared any tax at all, saving them an extra $320 million a year.

Surveys find that many Americans have things in mind to buy with their tax savings. Over the years the tax cut is calculated to bolster consumer spending, by some $25 billion to $30 billion a year from the current rate of about $375 billion a year.

### New Jobs Expected

The tax cut also will produce paychecks where none exist, backers contend. By "freeing the economy to move ahead more rapidly," the Treasury says, it will "create the millions of jobs that will be urgently needed in the years ahead."

Unemployment has been running at about 4 million, or 5.5 per cent of the work force, and the prospect of a net addition of about 1.4 million workers to the force annually after 1965 threatens to make unemployment even more acute; of last year's one million extra job seekers, one in six failed to find work. The Administration hopes the tax cut will help bring unemployment down to 5 per cent by year-end.

Businesses should get to keep about $1.5 billion they would otherwise have paid in taxes this year, and about $2.3 billion annually in future years, and officials figure they also have plenty to spend it on. Adjusted for price changes, business spending on plant and equipment declined about 1 per cent from 1957 through 1962, while Federal spending calculated on that "real" basis rose 13 per cent and consumer spending went up 17 per cent.

Considering also the investment tax credit and depreciation reform of 1962, Treasury Secretary Dillon has estimated that a new investment after the cut will be "more than a third" more profitable than one made before the changes. Officials reason the tax cut thus will spur investment in new and more efficient plants and equipment. . . . In calculating what the tax cut will do to the Government's income, official statements contend that "at no time will tax revenues fall below present levels," despite the rate cuts. It is explained that this is because the extra money circulating in the private sector will lift taxable profits and wages enough to make up for the lower rates.

Even with the tax cut, the President's budget for the next fiscal year, starting July 1, counts on receipts rising to $93 billion from $88.4 billion this fiscal year. Of the $4.6 billion increase, individual income tax payments are slated to provide $1 billion and corporate taxes $2.1 billion, with the rest coming from excises, customs duties and miscellaneous sources. With estimated spending shaved to $97.9 billion from $98.4 billion, the budget deficit is to shrink to $4.9 billion from $10 billion. These estimates could be altered by the cut's coming about a month later than budget-makers planned, however; that might reduce the deficit by close to $1 billion this fiscal year, though adding that much to next year's deficit.

Over two or three years, the planners concede, there will be a "shortfall" in Federal revenue of about $5 billion to $7 billion from the levels to which revenues would have risen without the tax cut. But by the fiscal year ending June 30, 1967, receipts should be $20 billion higher than the $88.4 billion estimated for this fiscal year, they say, and it is suggested the budget may be in balance around that time. If it weren't for the tax cut, whatever party is in power probably would have to step up Federal spending and deepen deficits over the next few years to try to pull the nation out of a recession, Administration men have argued.

## IV. THE RECKONING

### EDITOR'S INTRODUCTION

What the Johnson Administration—and the growing ranks of "new economists"—sought to accomplish with the income tax cut of 1964 and the excise tax cut of 1965 they succeeded in doing. In some ways the first article in Section I, above, is a catalog of those attainments.

Impressive as that achievement was, it was fortunate in its timing. The economy, as articles in Section II point out, was working well below full capacity. Hence the Administration could turn loose all its incentives to spur demand without concerning itself about overheating the economy.

But that situation changed markedly in the last months of 1965. Unemployment dwindled to a point where many categories of skilled workers such as tool- and diemakers, machinists, and engineers, were in very short supply. Many industries were working at full capacity. The aluminum industry, for example, was producing metal in greater quantities than its equipment was supposed to—in short, the mills were working at more than 100 per cent of rated capacity.

In many ways this is a classic—and dangerous—situation. As demand outstrips the economy's ability to produce, a very simple and ancient law of economics takes over—prices rise. The skilled workers who are now so much in demand ask, and get, higher wages. Similarly, aluminum producers struggling to keep up with a flow of orders can raise prices with full certainty that they will still sell all they can make. The result is inflation—a situation where the buying power of the dollar grows smaller and smaller.

How can this dilemma be avoided? Quite simply, by reversing the machinery used to spur the economy: higher interest rates for borrowing; higher taxes; and, perhaps, a cut in Federal Government spending. All these would have the effect of reducing the amount of money being spent and this in turn would reduce total demand.

The trick is to do it just enough so that demand drops only to the level of the economy's ability to fill it without undue strain. And as it turned out in 1966, this is a most difficult trick indeed.

The articles in this section deal solely with the economic events of 1966, for during that year the economy went from one in which demand and supply were in balance to a situation where demand was rapidly outdistancing supply. It is a kind of situation that will occur time and again in the future—or so long as there is a market economy in which supply and demand interact.

At the same time, 1966 also disclosed some of the weaknesses of the "new economics" and especially of using taxes as a tool. These weaknesses, which stem from technical requirements of changing the tax rate, and from human nature itself, will undoubtedly make their appearance in years to come. Thus the year 1966 is a model of some of the dangers which can crop up in using flexible economic policy and which we will have to bear in mind in comparable situations that will unquestionably arise again and again.

The first article, from *Business Week,* reflects the proper note of caution among economists at the beginning of 1966. The economy was heading into uncharted waters but there was no cause for alarm. Edwin L. Dale's article, written just a month and a half later, notes the first serious concerns over possible inflation. By May, as the *Wall Street Journal* article that follows points out, the concern had grown into a full-scale national debate. Roughly half the economists were saying "Don't do a thing" while the other half were demanding a tax increase to slow the economy.

The fourth article, from *U.S. News & World Report,* describes some of the difficulties which had cropped up. Because no fiscal, i.e. tax, restraints were applied, the brunt of holding back the galloping economy fell upon monetary policy—and it almost buckled. Interest rates were at their highest in forty years. For some people money was simply not available. Some economists—with the wisdom of hindsight—now say that during September of 1966 the

United States had a full-scale monetary crisis and the nation was on the verge of a financial panic.

President Johnson ultimately stepped in and proposed two measures that in effect amounted to a tax increase. This helped restore confidence and tensions began to subside. But there remained gnawing questions. What went wrong? In the last article of this section Mr. Dale, who has identified himself as an admirer of the new economists, shows how their theories collided with some unpredictable realities.

## AT THE CROSSROADS [1]

It was easy for economists to be right over the past five years. The next five, though, will be tougher.

The problems the economy has faced since 1960 were suited ideally to a kind of analysis long available to the profession. John Maynard Keynes thirty years ago showed how to stimulate a sluggish economy back to full employment. And for the past few years economists have been overjoyed that they could finally put these policies into practice. The result has been the longest U.S. peacetime expansion on record. For the once-obscure profession, it has meant a position of prominence never dreamed of before.

But now the economy has gone beyond problems for which Keynes had the answers. The United States has entered a post-Keynesian era where the main problem is how to combine steady growth at full employment with stable prices—a job much more difficult than closing the $50-billion gap between actual and potential gross national product that confronted policymakers in 1961.

### I. Brain Gathering

How to cope with this problem dominated last week's convention of the American Economic Association, which brought thousands of government, academic, and business economists to the New York Hilton for three days of conferences, speeches, and pro-

[1] Article, "The Slippery Path of Prosperity." *Business Week.* p 70-3. Ja. 1, '66. Reprinted from the January 1, 1966 issue of *Business Week* by special permission. Copyrighted © 1966 by McGraw-Hill, Inc.

fessional chitchat. Among those present were men who helped create the current expansion, and they are convinced that some post-Keynesian lessons learned in the past five years will help maintain price stability and low unemployment.

As Yale University's James Tobin, a member of President Kennedy's original Council of Economic Advisers (CEA), explains:

> A most encouraging thing is that we are operating at higher levels of utilization than in the mid-1950's with nothing like the wage-price pressures we had then. We're still not sure precisely what the trade-off between lower unemployment and inflation is, but there is evidence that the jobless rate can go lower than previously thought, without triggering inflation.

Walter W. Heller, head of the CEA from 1961 to 1964 and a major architect of the expansion, credits the improved environment to three factors: increased business investment, which should help industry bear up under added demand; increased human investment through training programs, which helps expand the labor force; and wage-price guidelines, which seem to have injected a sense of responsibility into private wage-price decisions. But even with these advantages over the 1950's, no economist at the convention treated lightly the problem of keeping the current boom under control.

This dilemma shows up most clearly in contrasting the chore facing the CEA under Gardner Ackley, its current chairman, with what the CEA faced in 1961. Says one former CEA staffer: "Heller had it easy; Ackley has it tough."

The primary reason is that quantitative problems have become more important and difficult. Up through 1965, the CEA had to package and sell old ideas—and at this they were genius. Heller and his colleagues debated the minority of economists who opposed the 1964 Revenue Act. And the CEA turned Keynes' weighty works into understandable and lively concepts that businessmen and politicians could understand. They struck away at old fiscal prejudices. They educated congressmen into cutting taxes at a time the budget was in deficit and the economy was well out of the shadows of the 1960-1961 recession.

## II. New Uncertainties

But now, the economy is so close to full employment, with Vietnam a major question, that prescribing the direction of policy is difficult and knowing how far to move in either direction is even rougher. As Ackley warned the convention, "The macroeconomics of a high employment economy is insufficiently known for us to map that path with a high degree of reliability."

When Heller took office in 1961, the gap between potential and actual GNP was enormous, unemployment was high, and industry was operating far below preferred rates. The quantitative problems of policy prescription were simple, and theoretical problems had been vanquished years before.

Says Gerhard Colm, chief economist of the National Planning Association, "In 1961, there couldn't be too much demand injection. Government could only do the right thing. Now, though, policy must be concerned with finer detail." Colm was one of the first to put flesh on the bones of Keynesian ideas in the United States.

Probably the most critical detail today relates to the size and capacity of the labor force. Labor is the limiting factor that already is causing concern, and it's something about which the Government can do little for the short run.

It's important now for the CEA to know where skilled labor bottlenecks are likely to appear; how many new workers (the so-called hidden unemployed) will rejoin the labor force when joblessness drops and improved job opportunities proliferate; and how much unemployment will persist in spite of growing demands for labor.

The increased importance of such detail worries economists. "We really don't know much yet about projections and predictions," says Charles J. Hitch, who is credited with introducing cost-effectiveness analysis into the Pentagon when he was Assistant Secretary of Defense. Now vice president of business and finance at the University of California, Hitch says, "Our analytical techniques are still quite crude, and improvements have been marginal."

At full employment, predictions become critical as policy-makers walk the edge between full potential growth and inflation. Thus, problems that have been behind the curtain for years came under serious discussion at the convention—such as the need to be flexible in both fiscal and monetary policy, the usefulness of "jaw-bone" (or persuasion) policy—particularly the guidelines—and the mobility and quick development of human resources. Economists have no definitive solutions for such full employment problems. Says Ackley, the need for answers is "urgent."

### III. Old Pressures

Moreover, policymakers now face more ticklish political problems than their predecessors did in the early 1960's. Economists worry that it was easier to sell expansionary fiscal measures like tax cuts than it will be to sell the restrictive measures that may be needed next. In fact, if there was any general accord among academic economists last week, it was that a tax increase rather than a slowdown in Great Society outlays would be the best way to reduce demand.

Economists press this issue, not in moral or social terms, but for strictly economic reasons. The basic argument is one of efficiency, says Heller. By enlarging the supply of usable manpower, the economy increases its potential growth rate and enlarges its room to expand without running into inflationary bottlenecks.

In purely economic terms, says Heller, "the payoff on a $2 billion or $3 billion investment in people is bigger than the payoff for a few billion dollars of low-priority consumption or business investment."

Many economists see the tax increase as a way to achieve another objective: Giving the President discretionary power to increase tax rates. Both Johnson and Kennedy wanted discretionary power to reduce taxes temporarily in case of recession; but Congress steadfastly maintained a jealous monopoly of its fiscal powers. But this time the request is for power to raise taxes—not reduce them—and for this unpopular task, Congress may be more willing to let the President do the dirty work alone.

Fiscal policy, of course, is not the only tool of Government control. Nearly all the academic economists at the convention vigorously backed the cooperative expansionary role that monetary policy has played over the past five years. Some also argue that the Federal Reserve Board could help dampen demand in inflationary periods, as the recent rise in the discount rate attempts to do.

But during the Korean conflict and World War II, the Fed pegged the Government bill rate to keep the cost of the debt as low as possible. If Vietnam meets with the same reaction, one economist warned, monetary policy will have its hands tied, and the Government will have no recourse other than fiscal policy.

Wage-price guidelines also won applause as a weapon in the Government's anti-inflation arsenal, and in general it was felt they have worked surprisingly well. Several economists, though, think the guidelines may need reinforcement as inflationary pressures mount, perhaps by giving them congressional as well as Executive backing.

Another anti-inflationary measure that drew interest was increased flexibility in the labor market. Arthur F. Burns, former head of President Eisenhower's CEA, believes computers and telephones could be used together to enable a man to walk into a local employment office, express his job preference, and be referred "in a matter of hours, if not minutes" to a list of jobs. Employers, too, could use such a service.

Not all the time at the convention was spent looking toward Washington. Introspection was a dominant theme of many speeches and less formal talk. The most damning criticism came from the University of Michigan's Kenneth E. Boulding who views the profession's performance in the past five years with misgivings.

Boulding is particularly upset by neglect of the impact of defense on the economy. "We must puncture the illusion that spending billions of dollars on the military each year makes us rich," he warned. A leading Quaker, Boulding pointed out that a major change in the economy over the past twenty-five years is that "defense industries have gone from 1 per cent to 10 per cent of GNP, but hardly anyone in the profession has paid attention to its impact."

Boulding's efforts to rechannel economic research won support from others. While the directions differed, there seems to be mounting impatience with academic research—particularly narrow, mathematical exercises—that serve no practical purpose.

Many agreed with George Jaszi, director of the Commerce Department's Office of Business Economics. He feels that although holes in the data still exist, there is enough information now for work to proceed in critical areas of Government policy—such as determinants of investment, the sources of economic growth, and the proper balance between consumption and investment, wages and profits.

This doesn't mean that economists want to limit themselves to policy-oriented questions. In fact, growing use of cost-analysis and operations-research techniques in business and government represented a proud feather worn at the convention. And even the practical areas that Jaszi suggests involve theoretical work rather than mere policy proposals. "We need better economic theory and also better methods of statistical inference," says Jaszi. "It would be a big mistake to assume that lack of facts is now the main bottleneck."

It's clear that economists themselves are grimly realistic about the difficulties ahead. However, they fear that the public is not, and this is the irony of the current expansion. It has taken economists decades to reach the pedestal of respectability where they now stand. It would take much less time to fall off.

Says Massachusetts Institute of Technology's Paul A. Samuelson, one of the first New Frontiersmen. "The public, I'm afraid, is asking for a perfection that isn't possible."

Nevertheless, more perfection than previously, now seems likely. Says Heller, "We've moved from a recession-prone to a recession-repellant period. The Government will be much more active and on top of the situation from now on."

Even Milton Friedman, leader of the conservative Chicago school, agrees with liberal economists that the profession should rethink its concept of what a recession is.

## THE FIRST WARNINGS [2]

The Government's economic policy, which has been such a conspicuous success in bringing the nation close to full employment and full prosperity, is under the heaviest criticism in years. Though the critics use different words, they all say essentially the same thing: The policy for this year risks serious inflation—the first serious inflation since the mid-fifties, and possibly the worst since the Korean War.

As the avalanche of Government statistics pours in, week after week, the critics' case begins to look stronger. But the Johnson Administration, for the time being at least, is hanging on. It is not changing policy, and its top officials still believe there is a good basis for their hope that serious inflation this year can be avoided —that is, an inflation noticeably worse than last year's 2 per cent average price increase.

The Government's policy is a frank gamble. It has operated for four years on the proposition that the nation had high unemployment and sluggish growth because total demand—total spending power—was insufficient. It pumped up demand by cutting taxes and raising Government spending, and by keeping monetary policy—the control of credit and the money supply—expansionary.

But everyone, including the Government knew there would come a point where the nation had reached its capacity to produce —its capacity of manpower and its capacity of plant. At that point, still more spending could not add to jobs and to the use of idle machines, but could only drive up prices.

### Great Debate

The great debate of 1966 is essentially over the answer to the single question: Are we at that point?

The Government, through the President's Economic Report to Congress last month, gave the negative answer. It said the country is not yet at full employment of manpower, nor at, or likely this year to reach, full utilization of plant capacity. Thus moderate

[2] Article, "The Other Big Question Is: Will the Economy Overheat?" by Edwin L. Dale, Jr., New York *Times* correspondent specializing in economic affairs. New York *Times*. p E6. F. 20, '66. © 1966 by The New York Times Company. Reprinted by permission.

additional stimulus for the economy is warranted, though the program moves "toward" restraint.

The critics, led by some leading Republican economists such as Arthur F. Burns and Neil H. Jacoby, answer the key question in the affirmative. They say the economy is already at capacity. Thus any additional stimulus is bound to run up prices. The right policy would be one of outright restraint, through lower Government spending, higher taxes or tighter money, or all three.

What, then, is the evidence up to now?

The President's Council of Economic Advisers cites such facts and expectations as these:

In the final quarter of last year the nation's factories were operating on the average at about 91 per cent of capacity, still a shade below the rate of 92 per cent that industry says it prefers without feeling strain. Equally important, business plans to expand capacity by a huge 7 per cent this year, which "should keep the average operating rate essentially unchanged from 1965."

### No Immediate Danger

There are still no "general" labor shortages, and another million teenagers will come on to the labor market this year, most of whom will not be in the armed forces. All in all, "our labor markets will be able to support a large further expansion of the economy," and the nation can safely reduce unemployment below its present level of 4 per cent.

Next, monetary policy has taken a distinct turn toward tightening. Even though the Administration opposed this move when it was taken early last December, it is now accepted as one means of checking an excessive increase in demand.

Interest rates have risen almost across the board—a situation dramatically reflected this week when the Government had to raise the interest rate on savings bonds from 3.75 to 4.15 per cent in order to attract savers.

And finally, the budget is at least moving in the direction of less stimulus, if not to the point of outright restraint this year. This is accomplished chiefly by a large increase in receipts.

The critics start with the facts as they exist, above all what has been happening to prices.

The key index is that of wholesale prices, which best reflects the pressure of demand on supply. This index has risen by the disturbing rate of one half per cent per month for three months in succession.

Next, the critics point to the nation's money supply. They concede that interest rates are now higher than before but they say this simply reflects the huge demand for credit. The Federal Reserve Board, they argue, has continued to supply the banking system with enough funds to produce an inflationary rate of increase in bank deposits and currency.

Finally, the critics emphasize the nonrestrictive nature of the budget, particularly for this calendar year. The budget can be measured in several ways, but nearly everyone concedes that it will apply some further stimulus this year.

After concluding that the Government's over-all program has pumped and will pump too much extra demand into the economy, the critics say with one voice that the voluntary anti-inflation "guideposts" will be almost completely ineffective in stemming the tide. Their view received some support this week as both construction and coal mining unions disclosed that they had no intention of abiding by the guideposts—which limit wage increases to 3.2 per cent—in their contract demands this year.

## Possible Cooling

This week's indicators were mixed. The big Social Security tax cut sharply into personal income, and hence spending power, in January, and for the fourth consecutive week the money supply failed to increase. These signs hinted at a possible cooling of the situation. But continuation of booming conditions showed up in another strong rise in January in both industrial production and new orders for durable goods.

Suppose the Government economists, as the figures come in, have to concede they were wrong and that serious inflation is present? They are no more willing to tolerate an inflation at an annual rate of 3 per cent or more for any extended period than are the critics.

The President has said, "I am convinced that we should levy higher taxes rather than accept inflation—which is the most unjust and capricious form of taxation."

Thus if the Government decides to act—probably no earlier than May—it will almost certainly propose a tax increase. Its experts are already working out what kind of a tax increase. They appear to be agreed—along with many private economists—that the best anti-inflation tax measure would be an across-the-board increase, as "neutral" as possible among income groups, in the income tax, accompanied by an increase in the corporation tax.

In any event, if the President eventually does decide to increase taxes, the reaction in Congress will provide a test of whether it accepts the proposition that the "New Economics" can work both ways, and also a test of whether Congress can act rapidly on a tax bill proposed for economic stabilization purposes.

## THE GREAT DEBATE [3]

To boost or not to boost?

That is the question—at least as far as taxes are concerned. It is a question causing remarkable dissension at the top levels of Government. In recent days, for instance, Federal Reserve Board Chairman William McChesney Martin has come out for a boost and Treasury Secretary Henry H. Fowler has come out against one, at least for now. The tax issue is also having repercussions on Wall Street, with many analysts citing the threat of an increase as a factor in the stock market decline.

Where do a majority of the nation's economic experts stand?

Behind the silver-haired chief of the Treasury, according to a *Wall Street Journal* survey of more than fifty prominent economists at universities, nonprofit research organizations and banks. Well over half, but by no means all, say they oppose any Federal tax increase at this time—for reasons that boil down to the conviction

[3] Article, "Debate Over Taxes." *Wall Street Journal.* p 1. My. 17, '66. Reprinted by permission.

that business activity is not currently so fast-paced as to generate dangerous price inflation.

## A Big Dissent

The substantial minority who favor a tax boost now—about 40 per cent of those interviewed—generally do so in the belief that the long expansion indeed is overheating and that something must quickly be done about it; the practical solution, these analysts contend, is an immediate tax increase.

The considerable disagreement among experts about the matter of taxes, the interviews further show, reflects a more fundamental disagreement over the general state of the U.S. economy; there is a broad consensus that a tax increase indeed would dampen business and check any rapid rise of prices.

The view generally put forward by the majority of analysts opposing a tax increase now is expressed by Albert T. Sommers, vice president and director of economic research at the National Industrial Conference Board, a nonprofit business research group in New York City:

The problems of inflation are diminishing. The economy has been overheated for a long time, but a lot of the steam is coming out of it now. [He adds] For a long time, the stimuli had been running way ahead of the restraints. But now the restraints have caught up; there's been a rise in the Social Security tax, an acceleration of corporate tax payments and individual withholding taxes, and money is at its tightest in a third of a century.

## Autos and Housing

Mr. Sommers warns that "we shouldn't expect that this long expansion won't finally run into a loss of energy. The auto industry is beginning to show this now, and the housing market is no better than stable."

Still more strongly opposed to a tax boost now is Roy E. Moor, vice president and economist of Fidelity-Philadelphia Trust Company, and formerly an economist for the Joint Economic Committee of Congress. The boom already is cooling, claims Mr. Moor, and "I see the seeds of a downturn in 1967." He adds that he detects "pretty clear evidence of where large firms are beginning to cut back very slightly on plans for new investments."

This impression, he says, grows out of "a whole series of discussions with economists in industrial firms who are beginning to have increased reservations about how much their companies should spend" in coming months.

To be sure, many of the economists who oppose a tax increase at present hasten to add that events later in the year could change their view. The big imponderable is Vietnam. Typically, A. Gilbert Heebner, vice president and economist of the Philadelphia National Bank, cautions that "very much depends on Vietnam. If defense spending levels off, we might get by without a tax increase." On the other hand, he indicates, a sharp step-up in the Vietnam fighting could necessitate a tax boost.

### Dispute Slowdown Idea

Authorities who want a tax boost immediately generally dispute the idea that the economic pace shows signs of slowing.

"We should have a tax increase—and soon," urges James Hund, dean of the school of business at Emory University in Atlanta. "I'm worried about inflation."

Norman Robertson, economist for Mellon National Bank & Trust Company, Pittsburgh, agrees: "We do have inflation—it's here now. All this nonsense of citing one economic indicator or another as indicative that we don't have it is simply statistical sophistry."

Unless the brakes—in the form of a tax increase—are immediately applied, there will be serious economic repercussions, probably next year, Mr. Robertson warns.

If a tax increase eventually is imposed, what form should it take?

Robert S. Einzig, a professor of economics at the University of California at Berkeley says:

I would recommend a $7 billion boost, applying equally to personal and corporate incomes. [He further suggests that] Congress should give the President standby authority to raise taxes, so we don't have to be concerned about waiting for Congress to debate about how much the increase should be. Just his having this power would have a sobering effect on the economy. . . . The boosts could be explicitly temporary.

Some economists would increase income taxes less sharply—
$5 billion is a figure frequently mentioned. But they also would
reduce or eliminate the 7 per cent tax credit that businessmen now
are allowed on new plant-and-equipment expenses.

"Capital expansion is one of the most ebullient areas of the
economy these days, and this would strike at the heart of the matter," declares William A. Tongue, an economist who teaches at
the University of Illinois.

## THE CRISIS [4]

The United States has appeared to many experts on finance to
be heading for a real money crisis.

On September 7 [1966], the president of the American Bankers
Association, Archie K. Davis, warned at White Sulphur Springs,
West Virginia, that tight money "over a long period of time could
precipitate a crisis."

Other bankers and economists told *U.S. News & World Report*
that a "financial panic" was a distinct possibility, unless the Government did something to relax the squeeze on credit and stop the
upward spiral of interest rates.

On September 8, President Johnson, reacting to just such warn-
ings, sent Congress a program to reduce borrowing by industry and
by the Government. The question still to be resolved: Will this
plan now solve the money problem that was worrying the nation's
financial leaders?

That worry has grown out of an acute shortage of money available for borrowing in relation to demands for money on the part
of those who want to build houses, invest, expand inventories, or do
any of the many things borrowers do with money.

When money for borrowing becomes difficult to find, those
wanting and needing to borrow tend to scramble for funds and bid
up the price of money—the interest rate. Interest rates today are
at the highest level in about forty years.

[4] From "Is a 'Money Crisis' Near?" Reprinted from *U.S. News & World Report.*
61:29-31. S. 19, '66.

## Why the Shortage?

The shortage of money is, in one sense, the result of a deliberate policy of the nation's money managers—members of the Federal Reserve Board—who are not supplying enough funds to banks to let them meet all demands for credit.

In another sense, the shortage is the result of the boom in business, which has whetted the appetites of corporations, farmers and consumers for more and more spending with borrowed money.

The purpose of the Reserve Board's tight-money policy is to curb that demand, which lies behind the spreading price inflation. Some in the financial community warn that the money situation has become so taut that any further tightening of the screws—or some unexpected development—might precipitate a crisis.

Already, savings and loan associations in many cases are out of money to lend for construction or to finance sales of older houses. The savings and loan industry had to pay out $1.5 billion more than it took in during July, as investors withdrew funds to spend or invest elsewhere at higher rates of return.

Banks face the need to pay off huge amounts of certificates of deposit falling due month by month. Banks often are having to deny loans to any but old customers. A statement from the Reserve Board on September 1 urged banks to ration funds even more strictly among the would-be borrowers.

There are complaints that small businessmen, lacking long-established banking connections, already are caught in a "crisis" of their own. The Government recently opened the credit tap wider at the Small Business Administration to help this group.

Insurance companies, by and large, have already entered into contracts to lend just about all the funds they will have available for lending for the rest of this year and much of 1967. In some cases, commitments extend into 1968.

H. W. Tatlock, vice president and treasurer of the Prudential Insurance Company of America, in Newark, New Jersey, said that about 50 per cent of the funds the company can expect to invest in "term loans" to business in 1967 will already be committed by the end of 1966.

"This is considerably more than normal," Mr. Tatlock said. He added that a "not inconsiderable" portion of the funds expected in 1968 has also been committed to old customers able to wait that long to get their money.

In Boston, William C. Whittemore, treasurer of the John Hancock Mutual Life Insurance Company, said funds are "relatively fully committed for the next year or year and a half." There is still money which has been allocated for mortgages or policy loans that have not yet been designated for specific borrowers, but, even so, Mr. Whittemore said, the funds are tied up in advance more than has been true in other years.

Insurance companies find that people are calling on them more often for policy loans and are taking out money committed for mortgages faster than normal.

Banks, which sometimes carried "temporary" loans on construction for fairly long periods, are now closing out these loans promptly, forcing borrowers to turn to insurance companies for permanent financing. As a result, there is less money available in the insurance industry for other types of lending.

Both banks and insurance companies have been selling lower-yield bonds in order to get cash to relend at higher rates of interest to other borrowers. This selling has had a depressing effect on the bond markets.

Big borrowers usually have been able to get money from banks. Now the Federal Reserve has told banks that, if they continue to dump bonds, they will be met with a jaundiced eye when they come to a Reserve Bank for more funds. . . . William F. Butler, vice president and chief economist of Chase Manhattan Bank, commented:

I think there is some risk here of a big money squeeze and, in effect, a financial panic. However, I have great confidence that the Reserve Board will not permit that to develop.

But what if there should be a miscalculation?

There then could be a rush for liquidity. Everybody would try to get into a liquid position [Mr. Butler explained], and not everybody could. We've already seen some savings and loan associations having to sell mortgages to meet withdrawals by depositors. Some insurance companies might have to sell investments. Banks would be forced to call some loans.

## WHAT WENT WRONG? [5]

The "new economics" has fallen on hard times. Not the theory but the results. This has been a trying year for a group of men in Government whose management of the American economy once seemed, and was, brilliant. They have not changed, nor have their ideas. But the image of success has flown away.

President Johnson, in a performance reminiscent at once of *The Perils of Pauline* and of *Hamlet,* has acted at the last minute to rescue the situation. After agonized delay, he has asked Congress to take certain actions raising taxes on business—something that fits comfortably into one part of the new economics. The rescue may or may not work, but at least the President has shown he has accepted that, politics or no politics, modern economic policy must work both ways. It cannot always be stimulating.

It took the United States a long time to accept the joys, and benefits, of stimulus. Given what Walter Heller, probably the most famous modern Government economic adviser, called our "Puritan ethic," we could not believe that it could in some conditions be both good and painless for the Government to spend more and tax less.

We finally did accept it. And we benefited. But the new economics always said there was another side, when we might have to tax more and spend less. For eight anguishing months this year, Mr. Johnson and his men—even though they recognized the principle—hoped that this day had not arrived. They have already waited too long to avert a good deal of trouble.

Prices are going up—much more rapidly than in the period of near stability between 1958 and 1965. The stock market has been in a state of dazed paralysis. Interest rates have risen very rapidly,

[5] Article, "What Went Wrong? Another Look at the New Economics," by Edwin L. Dale, Jr., New York *Times* correspondent specializing in economic affairs. New York *Times* Magazine. p 50-1+. S 18, '66. © 1966 by The New York Times Company. Reprinted by permission.

to heights not seen since the early 1920's. Unions are scrambling for the largest wage increases in ten years, and a wave of strikes is a good possibility. The President's appeals for restraint and his guideposts for wage and price behavior are being widely ignored.

And, more important than all of these things, there is abroad in the land a general sense of unease about the economy and its management by the Government. The President's belated action may restore confidence that the Government knows what it is doing and is doing the right thing; as always, results will tell the story. But nothing that happens from now on can change the fact that we have been going through a bad patch, recognized not only by Wall Street but by economists of nearly all shades of opinion.

In a way, the sense of unease is paradoxical. By the usual measures of production, jobs and incomes, the economy is continuing to prosper, even to boom, and it is unlikely that any disaster impends. Stock markets and interest rates are not everything. But the feeling that things have gone wrong is well justified, partly because what has been happening this year could very well build up difficulty for the future.

This time of troubles for the new economics may turn out to have been a good thing—good above all for the men who manage economic policy in the Government. In their inner hearts, as distinct from their public pronouncements, the Henry Fowlers and Gardner Ackleys—not to mention the Lyndon Johnsons—are not really surprised at most of what has been happening. They are not fools and nothing in the new economics ruled out the current troubles.

These men had hoped to have the best of both worlds: full employment and stable prices, with a war on. They have not succeeded. The fault is not in the new economics, nor, perhaps, can one blame its practitioners for aiming at utopia. But their failure to achieve it may be a healthy lesson for both them and us. It has certainly been a lesson to the present writer.

The President's message belatedly proposing some action—and accepting in effect, that utopia is not for this world—may already indicate that the lesson is being learned, though some doubts remain about the precise nature of his proposals.

Before an attempt to describe what went wrong, the first matter
to get straight is just what the new economics is. As economists
never tire of pointing out, it is not really new—certainly not in the
literature since John Maynard Keynes enunciated it in the middle
thirties. But it was new to America, at least politically and psychologically, when it was first applied in a big way in 1963 and
1964.

The new economics says one thing. If unemployment and idle
productive capacity persist in an advanced economy, this evil can
be cured by manipulation of government spending and taxation;
more spending, less taxation to increase total demand in the economy. In these circumstances the fact of a deficit in the budget is
irrelevant; magically, spending more and taxing less will actually
reduce the deficit by creating more production and jobs, and hence
more revenues. And it works.

That is really all the new economics is, but it is a great deal.
If President Franklin Roosevelt had received the message, the Great
Depression would probably have been over in a year or two instead
of lasting nearly half a generation. It is at least possible that if
the Eisenhower Administration had accepted the idea during parts
of its eight years in power, we would not now be afflicted by some
of the remaining problems of chronic unemployment among Negroes. If the Kennedy Administration had cut taxes in 1961 (*along
with* the defense buildup which at that time raised Government
spending), we would not have had to wait four years to get down
to 4 per cent unemployment.

What the new economics demonstrated, when it was finally
applied, was that unemployment—for Negroes as well as whites,
for the unskilled as well as the skilled, automation or no automation—could and would be reduced by manipulation of the Federal
budget, *and that this manipulation did not have to be accompanied
by inflation.* Until about the middle of 1965, it should be remembered, prices were still essentially stable—the rise in the consumer
price index running at about 1.3 per cent a year, far less than in
almost all other countries, and wholesale prices showing almost no
increase at all, though there had been a slight tilt upward after
mid-1964.

What, then, went wrong?

What went wrong was not the new economics. It always envisaged the danger of a situation such as the present one and, as the President's message this month to Congress indicates, provided a remedy.

Nor can the troubles be blamed on a sudden abandonment by business and labor of a previous willingness to apply restraint and abide by the Government's wage-price guideposts. These, an incidental companion of the new economics, establish the principle that wages can safely rise, without adding to average costs, in line with the long-term trend of growth of productivity, or output per man-hour, which appears to be about 3.2 per cent a year. Some prices, where little productivity growth is possible (haircuts, for example) would then rise, but prices would fall in industries, such as electronics, where productivity growth is rapid, leaving the average price level stable.

Actually, the guideposts were invented to deal with a rather special situation, covering only a part of the economy and limited to a "twilight zone" in the business cycle between heavy unemployment at one end, when natural forces keep down wages and prices, and hyper-full employment at the other, when natural forces push and pull them up. The guideposts were designed to meet the alleged, and probably real, problem that can be created *before* full employment is reached by two factors: union bargaining power and "pricing power" in concentrated industries like steel and aluminum, through which the price level can be pushed upward even before there is a classic inflationary condition of excess demand.

For several years it appeared on the surface that the guideposts were working. Bargained wage settlements were not much above the 3.2 per cent level, and average industrial prices did remain stable. However, the main reason undoubtedly was that the natural forces of competition were producing results that happened to coincide with what the guideposts called for. Business had excess capacity—and prices are difficult to increase if a competitor is ready to grab the order. Unemployment reduced union bargaining power.          ↳ Cont.

Other industrial countries have found that voluntary restraint policies always prove ineffective as soon as full employment, or nearly full employment, is reached. Even Mr. Ackley and his embattled colleagues on the Council of Economic Advisers have conceded that the guideposts could not work in a condition of boom with excess demand and scarce labor. Their only contention this year—scoffed at by many of their professional fellows outside of Government—was that the economy had not yet reached that point.

The trouble, then, was not in the new economics. Nor was it in a shift from compliance with the guideposts to defiance of them by the power centers in the private economy.

Rather, what went wrong was that the men in charge let a good thing—expansion of total demand—go just too far. All of a sudden, they had nothing but trouble. They had a revival of inflation, and the absence of inflation was a keystone of the new economics and of American prosperity—both practically and psychologically. A grave danger toward the end of 1966 was that the whole modern idea of management of demand through the Government budget would be discredited.

With the inflation came the upward surge of interest rates and a condition approaching panic in the nation's money markets. Former President Harry S. Truman, who rarely speaks out on current events, said he feared the situation could lead to a "serious depression"—a remark that President Johnson felt he had to counter with some reassurance the next day.

How did it happen? To begin with, the men in charge had some very bad luck.

Picture the turn of the year 1964-65. The tax cut of early 1964 was clearly working. Unemployment had declined to within a tenth of a per cent of the Government's prediction. Much of the business community had swung to President Johnson in the election of November. The Congress that was elected was the most responsive to presidential initiative in thirty years.

Gardner Ackley and his associates on the Council of Economic Advisers duly examined early that winter the outlook for the year ahead. Using the same techniques that had provided the justification for the big 1964 income tax cut, and faced with a firm presidential decision that the spending side of the budget must be held within $100 billion, they concluded that total demand in 1965 would need a further boost through yet another tax cut—though smaller and of a different kind—to maintain the progress toward lower unemployment. Idle men and machines remained. Thus there was proposed, to congressional huzzahs, the excise tax cut of 1965, which swept away a host of nuisance taxes that had lasted for fifteen years and more—a tax reduction that added to total demand like any other.

The tax cut took effect May 1, 1965. The outlook was good for a continued balanced expansion of the economy. And then the President—perhaps one should say the ornery world—pulled the rug out from under everything.

Mr. Johnson, for reasons wholly unconnected with the economic situation, of course, announced the decision on July 28 that the United States would undertake a major military involvement in Vietnam. From that point on a persistent devil, uncertainty, poisoned the brew of economic policy.

Two things can be said about the economic effects of the war.

One is that it has had far less impact on our normal life, or on the economy, than any other war in modern times, whether measured by shortages of goods, the rise in prices, the maintenance of nondefense spending or any other test. The war, by itself, did not cause our troubles.

But the other is that it had just enough impact to knock into a cocked hat all the original careful calculations of the new economists.

For openers, they got poor estimates from Mr. McNamara's Defense Department of the probable monthly course of expenditures. For reasons known best to himself, and perhaps simply because even his computers are far from infallible, Mr. McNamara consistently underestimated the "add-on" to defense expenditures that was in the cards, or else refused to supply any precise estimate at all.

The amounts of the estimating error were not mammoth. But the essence of the new economics, at a time of prosperity, is its effort to manipulate total demand by amounts as small as $3 billion to $5 billion. When the economy is approaching full employment, amounts of this magnitude can be of crucial importance in the balance between stable prosperity and inflation, even though the total output of goods and services—the gross national product—is more than $700 billion. Mr. McNamara understated defense outlays for calendar year 1966 by this crucial margin. It now appears that military outlays this year will be about $62 billion, instead of the $58 billion estimated in the budget in January. Decisions affecting demand need more precision than that.

A related piece of bad luck stemmed from the persistent inadequacies of our statistics, even though they are the best in the world. At the time of decision on whether to shift policy away from stimulus of demand decisively toward restraint—roughly the four weeks sandwiching last Christmas—the indicators gave off slightly false signals. Mr. Ackley, not to mention the general public, had no clear idea of how exuberant the boom had really become and how suddenly the classic inflationary pressures of excess demand were emerging.

But, finally and most important, what went wrong was not bad luck but a bad decision—a decision by the President.

The problem was clear. The added demand caused by the war, coming at a time when unemployment was already down to 4 per cent of the labor force and factories were operating at about 91 per cent of capacity, threatened to swing the economy over from a condition of stable, relatively inflation-free prosperity to a condition of excess demand, when prices and then wages would spurt upward. The remedy for this condition was clear, and had always been envisioned by the new economics: higher taxes (given the President's decision that his domestic programs must be increased somewhat further, thus ruling out expenditure reduction).

Allowing for all the uncertainty about the exact magnitude of the increase in defense spending, and allowing for the somewhat foggy signals given off by the economic indicators, Mr. Johnson did not lack for advice to raise taxes. No man outside the Government can say with certainty at this point who advised what, and with what force. But it is likely that Mr. Ackley's Council of Economic

Advisers recommended a tax increase, and perhaps also Budget Director Charles L. Schultze, and that Treasury Secretary Fowler opposed it. Numerous outside experts felt it was advisable. The semi-independent Federal Reserve Board strongly favored it.

For this is the other part of the new economics: When demand is deficient, it should be stimulated; when demand is excessive, it should be restrained. The tax weapon is the most rapid and potent to accomplish either result.

It was possible to argue last winter, when the tax decision was being made, that the outlook was not clearly inflationary. It was not then known, for example, how big the surge of business investment in plant and equipment would be. There was some hope that the turn toward a tighter monetary policy by the Federal Reserve Board in early December—even though the move was criticized at the time by the President—would act as a restraining influence on total borrowing and hence total demand (in the event, it did not begin to work effectively until almost a year later, though the change did set off an upward spiral of interest rates while credit continued to expand).

The President also had to weigh the politics of the situation. It is not only that tax increases are always unpopular, but this one would be associated with a war that commanded something less than overwhelming support. Would Congress, having reduced taxes in each of the two previous years, go along?

In any event, the President made his decision in the negative. And he proceeded to compound the problem by adopting two gimmicks that made the budget look better but which did not restrain the exuberant economy and had the harmful side effect of running up interest rates even further. These were a speed-up in corporate tax collections (the corporations simply borrowed more to pay their taxes but did not reduce their investment in plant and equipment) and the sale of special Government "participation certificates" which did not count as Treasury debt but added substantially to the total demand for credit.

We can safely say, with hindsight, that the budget of last January [1966]—which set the basic policy of economic management for the year ahead—represented a set of thoroughly bad decisions.

The present writer would like to emphasize the word "hindsight," for at the time he was as uncertain of the right thing to do as the President evidently was. But it is as clear now as anything can ever be that if the President had decided the other way and raised taxes, a good deal of our present troubles would not have occurred, to say nothing of future troubles that may be impending.

The negative tax decision having been made, the Council of Economic Advisers put on a brave front. In the annual economic message to Congress in January the Council stuck to the guideposts and projected a year of comparatively stable prices, with an increase in the range of 2 per cent or less. More important, in his part of the message the President took explicit notice of the possible need for restraint in the form of a tax increase and said:

> If it should turn out that additional insurance is needed, then I am convinced that we should levy higher taxes rather than accept inflation—which is the most unjust and capricious form of taxation.

At least until September 8, eight months later, those were hollow words. It took a sizable amount of inflation before the President decided he had to redeem his pledge.

Secretary of the Treasury Fowler went around the country and before congressional committees warning against too much restraint, against "overkill" and "slamming on the brakes too hard." He left open the possibility of a tax increase, but kept saying things like this (in early May):

> Should the disturbing developments in the private economy turn out to be largely temporary, we were and remain concerned that tax increases could prove inappropriate and might disrupt our transition to a full employment level of growth in a balanced economy.

Chief economic adviser Ackley told the Congressional Joint Economic Committee that "our own judgment is that the combination of fiscal and monetary policies we now have is appropriate to the current situation and the outlook for the economy." And he told the Economic Club of Detroit that "the nation cannot afford an inflationary wage-price spiral."

No doubt these gentlemen were being genuine and, of course, there is no certainty in economics. But we all know what happened.

In a word, demand, unrestrained by a tax increase, continued to grow too fast.

Consumer prices since the beginning of the year have been rising at an annual rate of 3.5 per cent, wholesale prices a bit faster. This is by no means a raging inflation, and is in fact about in line with the price increases that many European countries have been accustomed to in normal prosperous years. But it changed the entire climate.

The guideposts began to crumble. Despite presidential intervention, the airline mechanics' union won a settlement raising wages by 5 per cent a year. And the worst of the wage problem is still ahead, for relatively few major contracts expired in the first part of this year.

As interest rates rose (without curbing total borrowing much), the stock market, classically, declined because investors could get such good returns by buying bonds. Uncertainty over the course of war spending, and what the President might do, added to the collapse of confidence. Other factors, such as jitteriness over the British pound and the international financial situation, played a role, but a feeling that the economy was not being managed with its former skill was undoubtedly a decisive element in the big decline.

The one real victim of the high interest rates, as had happened before, was the housing industry, and congressional protests mounted. Businesses were able to raise their prices, in most cases by relatively moderate amounts, and profits continued exceptionally high. But talk of a squeeze on profits, partly because of rising wage costs, began to revive.

Above all, the Government appeared to be floundering. As the months went on, it became clearer that taxes should have been raised; but doubts began to be expressed, even among economists who had advocated the step, whether it was not too late. The fear was that a combination of tight money and other factors was already working in the direction of a slowing down of the economy early in 1967, and thus a tax increase now might become an "overcure" (though some experts have continued to advocate a tax increase up to the present moment). The President openly confessed his uncertainty and simply continued, *ad nauseam,* to appeal for restraint.

Now that he has at last decided to act, doubts remain. He *may* be too late. His proposals, designed to curb the booming sector of business investment in plant and equipment by removing the tax subsidy on such investment, may have come along at a time when this sector was ready to cool off anyway. No one knows, and all that is certain is that a sizable number of businessmen, convinced that the 7 per cent tax credit on investment was to be a permanent part of the tax structure, are angry.

How bad, then, is the situation? An amusing, and perhaps revealing observation can be made about the human animal, in connection with the economic situation or anything else. Imagine a sort of "prosperity index" running from zero to 100. A great depression, with a quarter of the labor force out of work, might show an index figure of 50. There is a thoroughly justified general feeling of distress.

Then suppose, thanks in good part to effective management of demand by Government policy using the principles of the new economics, the index rises to 95, with nearly full employment and relatively stable prices. Finally, assume that the index then drops back to 92, as a few things go wrong, including a little inflation.

The fascinating thing is that there is almost as much wailing and gnashing of teeth when the index drops from 95 to 92 as when it was at 50. Not quite, but almost.

The fact is that, late in 1966, the American economy on the whole is doing very well. Unemployment among adults is down near rock bottom (only 2 per cent among married men). Factories are flush with orders and profits are at record levels. Incomes, taken as a whole, are rising rapidly, and still slightly faster than prices. And even the inflation has been only a third as great, to cite one comparison, as the rise in prices in the first year of the Korean war. Astonishingly, the vast American economy is carrying a very substantial war with only a minimal impact on "business as usual."

Thus, up to now at least, the situation is not really all that bad. But we may not yet have seen the worst consequences of the wrong decision of last January.

American postwar experience has been that every period of significantly rising prices and excess demand has been followed by a recession. There are well-known economic explanations for this process, involving the impact of inflation on such factors as inventory accumulation, overexpansion of plant capacity and monetary tightness. The problem is not a great depression, but a recession, which usually lasts about a year or a little less.

We may have to pay the price of a recession next year for the failure of the Government to act earlier this year through a tax increase to restrain excess demand. The stock market, which does not have a bad record as a forecaster when really major declines are involved, has certainly pointed that way.

Thus it is not only that inflation is undesirable because it works the well-known injustices on the aged and others living on fixed incomes. It also sets in motion forces that can bring on a slump, with rising unemployment.

As Senator Javits and others have pointed out, the worst thing that could happen in the long, slow struggle to improve the situation of the poor would be even a mild slump in the general economy. Yet that is what we may have, even with the war continuing.

We may not. A recession is not inevitable and the Administration's belated measures, assuming Congress approves them, may yet help to rescue the situation. Pauline may not be run over by the railroad train after all, and our situation is certainly not, and has not been, desperate. Total demand in the economy is continuing to expand, and may now grow at more sustainable pace.

But even if we avoid a recession, the general confidence of the public in effective governmental economic management has, understandably and legitimately, broken down. One of the casualties could be faith in the new economics, even though the real trouble this year was that the new economics was not applied soon enough.

A lesson, it is to be hoped, has been learned. Next time, the courage and the willingness to use the tax-increase weapon against over-exuberance and excess demand may be greater. People, after all, can learn from their mistakes.

But the fact remains that Mr. Johnson goofed badly last January —and the chickens are coming home to roost.

## V. THE HUMAN ELEMENT IN TAXATION

### EDITOR'S INTRODUCTION

In "What Went Wrong?" [see preceding section], Edwin L. Dale observed that one reason things went wrong in 1966 was that the Administration failed to act as decisively as it might have.

But the Administration is made up of men who have shortcomings, personal interests, and biases as all men do. These human elements play perhaps an even greater role in the formulation of economic policy than economic theory—and they are one reason why knowledgeable economists usually refer to the "political economy" when they discuss economic policy instead of simply calling it the "economy."

The first three articles in this section focus on the human considerations in taxation and the impediments these can pose when taxes are used as an economic tool. The last article examines the technical shortcomings of the new economics.

The first article is a history of the conflict between direct and indirect forms of taxation. The salient point is that because taxes are paid by people there is a natural rivalry among interest groups, each of which tries to shift the burden onto another group. This rivalry hasn't changed much in modern times, as the second article points out. An outgrowth of the national focus on taxes during the early 1960's was an effort to revise the tax system and eliminate some of the more conspicuous loopholes that some interests had been able to make for themselves. The article concludes that, for all intents and purposes, the more powerful groups succeeded in keeping their loopholes.

The extreme difficulty of deciding which of a variety of taxes to impose or rescind in order to slow down or speed up the economy is illustrated in the next article, which gives a detailed account of the agonizing political and economic soul-searching that went on in the White House before it initiated legislation (later passed) to raise certain taxes in the fall of 1966.

The last selection considers some technical shortcomings of the new economics. Although few economists now dispute the basic assumptions of Keynesian economics, many seriously question their excessive application on a short-term basis. In this article Dr. Beryl Sprinkel, a bank economist, argues that the data available to us now are not adequate for making rapid-fire changes in economic policy and that, in any case, rapid-fire changes destroy the confidence necessary for a smoothly working economy.

## DIRECT VERSUS INDIRECT TAXATION [1]

With the introduction of direct taxation, the progressive increase of public revenues becomes far easier. This is fortunate, for with the advance of civilization the public expenditures grow apace. For a long time, as we have seen, almost the only aims of government are security and defense. But as economic conditions develop and various classes of society differentiate, more attention must be paid to matters of general welfare. Expenditures for commerce, industry and transportation arise. The need is felt for better roads, for more canals, for improved methods of communication through the postal service. Then the less material ends of government are recognized. Education must be provided, hospitals and asylums must be erected, and the sanitary conditions must be looked after. Finally comes the immense growth of the modern state, with its new functions due partly to the industrial revolution, partly to the growth of democracy, partly to the recognition in legislation of the preventive as against the repressive principle. These new functions mean fresh expenditures; and these expenditures mean increased taxes. Thus the characteristic mark of the modern age is taxation as against the more or less self-sufficing public economy of former times.

Direct taxation, as we have seen, generally forms the last step in the historical development of public revenues. At first regarded entirely as an extraordinary means of support, it gradually assumes the character of an ordinary form of revenue. In the early days of classic

[1] From *Essays in Taxation*, by Edwin R. A. Seligman. Macmillan. New York. '25. p 7-9. Reprinted by permission. The late author was McVickar Professor of Political Economy at Columbia University and an authority on taxation.

antiquity the direct tax was used only in very exceptional exigencies and was, in fact, regarded as a compulsory loan, to be repaid in the future. It was not until after the establishment of the Roman Empire, for instance, that the regular direct taxation of Roman citizens began. And the same process may be observed throughout the history of many medieval states down to the most recent period of European and American history.

In some cases, however, this historical process assumes a slightly different form. It depends entirely on the economic conditions and on the relative importance of the various social classes. For instance, it is incontrovertible that certain kinds of indirect payments always come first, as has been explained above. [See "The Development of Taxation" in Section III, above.] But when the people understand that indirect charges on commodities increase their price and thus form veritable taxes, it sometimes happens that more opposition is shown to indirect than to direct taxation. In such cases direct taxes furnish the ordinary revenue, and it is only after a severe struggle that indirect taxes are introduced.

This process can be clearly traced in the history of medieval and modern revenue. In democratic communities, where the legislation is influenced by the mass of the people, we commonly discern a tendency to oppose indirect taxes on consumption. In the early medieval towns the democratic instincts were strong, because of the more equal distribution of property. We accordingly find that the revenue system was based largely on direct payments, and that the populace rebelled against indirect imposts. But on the Continent, where aristocratic influences gradually became powerful enough to break down the communal liberty and democracy, the mass of the people were ground down by taxes on the necessaries of life, while the wealthier or governing classes practically escaped. When the democratic upheaval took place, as in the Italian towns, we find an attempt to reintroduce the old order of things and to reach the wealthy by a system of direct taxes. But with the downfall of the medieval democracy, the property and income taxes disappeared, while the *octroi* [tolls] and municipal indirect taxes again came to the front. Only in England, where the democratic instincts maintained themselves somewhat more strongly, and where the power of the aristocracy was held in check by a strong monarchy, do we find continued opposition to the general excises and to local taxes on the necessaries of life. It was with the greatest difficulty that the excise system was introduced. And the same feeling was awakened under similar conditions on the other side of the Atlantic, when Hamilton initiated his system of indirect taxation or internal revenue in the Federal fiscal system of the United States. "The time will come," said one of the members of Congress in 1790, "when the poor man will not be able to wash his shirt without paying a tax." With the advent of the modern democratic state, we notice the same tendency. Indirect taxes, says Lassalle [Ferdinand Lassalle, nineteenth century German Marxist], are taxes on labor. Hence the efforts of modern democracy in England, in Switzerland and in America to confine indirect taxes on consumption and exchange within the narrowest limits.

On the other hand, there is a countertendency which has frequently been overlooked. Curious as it may seem, indirect taxes were advocated in the later middle ages as the means of introducing not inequality, but equality, of taxation. This was owing to the fact that the privileged classes on the Continent had succeeded in securing virtual immunity from taxation. The nobles were largely exempted from the land tax, while the clergy and the wealthier citizens in general were able to a large degree to purchase freedom from the tax burdens. What was more natural than that the statesmen and tax reformers should attempt to make them pay something through taxes on their expenditure, which they could not well escape? Their plan, it is true, no longer took the shape simply of taxes on the necessaries of life; it was now expanded into the single tax on all expense which would reach the rich as well as the poor. This was the idea of Colbert [Jean Baptiste Colbert, seventeenth century French financial reformer]; and it has been the idea from the time of Hobbes [Thomas Hobbes, seventeenth century English political and social philosopher] and Petty [Sir William Petty, seventeenth century English political economist] of all enthusiasts for indirect taxation in England, and of many writers in Germany, in France and in Italy. Today we are clamoring for the abolition of indirect taxation; formerly the reformers clamored for a single universal indirect tax. The explanation, as we see, is simple.

But this does not yet answer the question why excise taxes were actually introduced into England, as elsewhere, in the seventeenth century. The fact is that tax reformers cannot do much good if economic conditions are not ripe for their proposals. It must be confessed that according to the experience of history most reforms, in finance at least, are due to selfish reasons; they are the necessary outcome of changes in economic relations and of the efforts of each class, whether it be the small or the large class, to gain some advantage for itself. The classic home of the excise tax or indirect tax on business and trade is Holland. It is well known that Holland, during the sixteenth and seventeenth centuries, had become the leading financial and trading nation of Europe. In the other countries wealth was still centered in the landed interests, and the whole system of taxation was largely dominated by feudal aristocratic ideas. The direct taxes were land taxes, because wealth consisted chiefly of land; but the landed proprietors sought to escape the burden by assessing real property as low as possible and by putting taxes on the necessaries of life of the poorer classes. In Holland, on the other hand, wealth was now largely centered in the moneyed interest. The great traders and merchants did not relish any direct taxation of trading capital, and therefore devised a system of indirect taxation of business which would, as they thought and hoped, be shifted to the community in general, and to the poorer classes in particular. Thus developed the stamp taxes, the excise taxes, and the whole host of indirect taxes for which Holland was noted.

The seventeenth century marks the rise of the trading class in England; "the glorious revolution" was a revolution not so much of the people as of what the Socialists love to call the "bourgeois." Puritanism and commercialism went hand in hand, and the downfall of the Stuarts not only put an end to feudalism, but weakened the fiscal ascendancy of the landowner—an ascendancy to which another serious blow was given by the abolition of the Corn Laws, and whose final overthrow in England, as elsewhere, is fast approaching. The indirect taxes of the seventeenth century were thus the outgrowth of the effort on the part of the commercial classes to escape the burdens which the landowners were desirous of placing on them. The selfish designs of the capitalists and the unselfish ideas of the tax reformers went hand in hand to widen the scope of indirect taxes. And as the trading class developed in the other countries, the system of excise spread with it. (A word may be said, in passing, about our present attitude toward indirect taxes. There is a prodigious amount of cant on this topic. Many thinkers are apt to make common cause with the Socialists and the single-taxers in demanding the complete abolition of the so-called indirect taxes. This is a mistake. There is nothing inherently bad about an indirect tax, nor is there anything inherently good about a direct tax. It depends entirely upon what kind of direct or indirect tax it is. A direct tax on the laborer is not necessarily good because it is direct; an indirect tax on the luxury of the rich is not necessarily bad because it is indirect. It happens, indeed, that most of the indirect taxes of the past have been devised by the powerful in order that their burden might fall on the weak; but it is by no means impossible to frame a system of taxes on consumption which will supplement other taxes and do substantial justice to all. . . .) It was not until the democratic movement of the nineteenth century, when the system of excises was recognized as a burden on the poorer classes, that the number of commodities subject to excise was gradually reduced.

## THE BATTLE GOES ON [2]

On the morning of last June 6 [1963], the House Ways and Means Committee, plodding slowly through the Administration tax-reform proposals, came, at last, to the hottest of hot potatoes: the oil-depletion allowance. But even before Treasury Department spokesmen could begin to explain their plan for a mild tightening of the special tax deductions enjoyed by the oil industry, a motion was made to bypass the entire subject without further debate. The motion—made, ironically, by California's Cecil King, usually a loyal Administration supporter with a "prolabor" voting record—

[2] From "The Slow, Quiet Murder of Tax Reform," article by Philip M. Stern adapted from material in his *Great Treasury Raid* (Random House. New York. '64). *Harper's Magazine.* 227:63-8. D. '63. Reprinted by permission of Curtis Brown, Ltd. Copyright © 1963 by Philip Stern. First published in *Harper's Magazine.* Mr. Stern is a free-lance writer who has served in the Interior and State Departments and other Federal agencies.

was quickly passed, the New York *Times* reported, "by near-unanimous voice vote." (Days later, after some unfriendly newspaper editorials, the Committee did reconsider, and approved a token part of the original depletion proposal.)

Perhaps other Kennedy loophole-closing proposals were less summarily treated by Ways and Means. But whatever amenities were observed, the outcome was, in most cases, as dismal. By August, even before Ways and Means had finished its work, the tax-reform program was so badly battered that the Administration threw in the sponge, electing to abandon the fight for tax reform in the hope of speedier passage of its tax-cut pep pill for the economy.

Yet as of early November, with Senate hearings proceeding at a desultory pace, it appeared the reforms may have been sacrificed in vain, for the strong possibility loomed that the tax bill would not be passed until early 1964.

To veteran observers of the tax-writing process, the mauling of the Kennedy reform program was no surprise. True, there were in 1963 some special inhibiting factors, prime among them the President's own declaration last February that nothing—including controversial reforms—"should stand in [the] way" of a tax cut (JFK SCUTTLED OWN TAX BILL was one headline). Yet most past loophole-closing efforts have met the same fate as the 1963 Kennedy round; in fact, the tax laws today contain far more preferences, exceptions, exclusions, and special advantages than existed five years ago, or ten or twenty—this despite an occasional tax-tightening here or there.

Judging by that evidence, the deck is heavily stacked against tax reform. Turning up a few of the cards in the deck discloses why:

*The proreform forces:* diffuse, inarticulate, politically impotent (who ever heard of an anti-depletion "lobby"?) . . .

*The antireform forces:* highly focused, intensely vocal, politically powerful . . .

*The tax-writing power in Congress:* tightly held by two carefully chosen committees . . .

*The complexity of the tax law:* supremely technical, it confounds many lawyers, perplexes most congressmen, totally baffles the public . . .

*The tax experts and lobbyists:* often they alone can find their way through the legal and verbal fog, which can shroud their actions from public understanding and scrutiny.

Each of these cards turns up not once but many times as a tax bill works its way through the legislative maze, and each played its part in the dismal defeat of the 1963 Kennedy reforms.

### Sixty-seven Witnesses for Oil

Hearings on the 1963 tax bill opened formally on February 6, when Treasury Secretary Douglas Dillon took his seat before the twenty-five Ways and Means Committee members arrayed above him on a semicircular dais, and laboriously unfolded the "comprehensive tax-reform" program the President had presaged two years earlier. It was, in scope at least, ambitious. Challenging many of the most powerful business lobbies in Washington, the Administration proposed stiffer taxes on oil, coal, real estate, timber, cattle, insurance, top corporation executives, and the privately owned corporations used as a tax shield by the very wealthy. It also risked the opposition of the labor unions' lobby by seeking to end, for example, the tax-free sick-pay privilege, which benefits working people. And by proposing a curb on tax deductions for such items as home mortgage interest and charitable gifts, the Administration flung a disastrously unpopular challenge not only to middle-income taxpayers, but also to such strong and vocal groups as churches, charities, and the home-building industry, which would be indirectly affected.

Douglas Dillon must have known he faced an uphill fight. He was but the first of 195 witnesses the Committee was to hear from in twenty-seven tedious days of hearings, recorded in 4,035 pages of testimony, and after he left the stand few other proreform voices were heard. The remainder of the hearings were, as usual, dominated by spokesmen for this industry, that company, this labor union, cautioning against one Administration proposal or another. For example, in the four days set aside for testimony on the oil-depletion recommendations, the Committee heard from no less than sixty-seven officials, individuals, and organizations, including thirteen governors and ten congressmen—not one favoring reform.

Washington's downtown office buildings are studded with listening posts for the various industries, ready to alert industry members to any dangers such as an adverse tax proposal. The ninth floor of the Commonwealth Building, for example, is occupied by the American Petroleum Institute, whose president—tall, striking Frank Ikard—can furnish the most authentic advice on how to pass or stymie tax measures: for seven years, as a Texas congressman, he was a member of the Ways and Means Committee. On the fifth floor of the modern Solar Building are the offices of the National Coal Policy Conference, headed by portly, bespectacled, soft-spoken Joe Moody, a seventeen-year veteran on the Washington scene. (Moody decided early in 1963 that the favorable tax treatment enjoyed by coal-royalty income was in no danger of repeal, as asked by the Administration, and so mounted no extraordinary national effort.) The real estate industry has its National Association of Real Estate Boards, and the National Association of Life Underwriters was watchful of proposals for stiffer rules on the taxation of group life insurance.

There is, of course, nothing reprehensible in an industry's maintaining a Washington representative or in sixty-seven proindustry witnesses bombarding the Committee. But the general public has no such watchdogs; and tax hearings are so lopsided that, as one close observer put it, Congress has difficulty securing "a balanced view of what is in the general interest, what the public wants, or what the public would want if it were informed of the facts." True, at scattered points in the hearing, the Administration's oil proposal did receive glancing support from Columbia Professor Roy Blough, from the American Veterans Committee, the National Farmers Union, and three unaffiliated witnesses; but as usual the Treasury Department's was the principal voice of tax reform.

Treasury, though, possesses little of the political power that Washington responds to. Unlike the Labor and Agriculture Departments, it lacks the political leverage of a constituency of its own, and, because it is chronically opposed to the special tax favors many lawmakers believe should be granted, it comes to be regarded not as representing the collective interests of all taxpayers, but as a stiff-necked, theory-minded bureaucracy insensitive to the real-life problems of flesh-and-blood taxpayers. Still, weak reed or strong, the Treasury is virtually all that the loophole-closers have to lean on.

## Capturing the Swing Votes

When the public hearings are finally concluded, the Ways and Means Committee descends from its dais and assembles around a U-shaped table to begin shaping the tax bill it will recommend to the House.

The commodious room in which it labors—by far the largest of the House hearing rooms—attests the fact that Ways and Means is the House's most powerful legislative committee. Looking down from the pale-green walls are the portraits of former Ways and Means chairmen, three of whom (Polk, Fillmore, and McKinley) later ascended to the White House. But as Chief Executives, their power on tax matters could hardly have been greater than when they were in Congress. One portrait is that of Robert L. ("Muley") Doughton, who once (1949) suffered the indignity of having his committee approve, by a one-vote margin, a bill inimical to his North Carolina tobacco constituency. Shaken but not downed, Mr. Doughton successfully insisted that the President of the United States not only reverse the official Administration position on the measure but also telephone a pro-Administration Committee member and request him to change his vote.

Ways and Means maintains a tight rein on all major tax, tariff, or Social Security legislation; for its assent is required, by House procedure, for any amendments to such bills to be introduced during floor debate. This tight committee control is crucial, for it permits pressure-group spokesmen to concentrate on a limited target. If they can win the favor of a few "swing" votes on Ways and Means, they can, by and large, ignore the other 400-plus members of the House. In 1963, when the ten Republican committee members were generally arrayed solidly against the Administration, as few as three Democratic defections could defeat any reform. Since any tax-tightening proposal was bound to touch the political nerve end of one Democrat or other, it required no special lobbying effort to put together a shifting antireform coalition to defeat one after another

of the Administration's recommendations. After all, how could
John Watts, from Kentucky, permit his colleagues to vote for stiffer
taxes on cattle and race horses? And how could such Administration
loyalists as Al Ullman, from timber-laden Oregon, or Pat Jennings,
from a coal-rich Virginia district, support higher taxes on timber or
coal?

One of the factors helping to solder the oil-depletion provisions
so securely into the tax laws has been the careful selection of Ways
and Means members. One recent candidate for Committee member-
ship was "approached" (he declines to say by whom) for a commitment in favor of oil depletion and was told that all the other
contestants for the seat had declared themselves prodepletion, just as
all prior-year candidates had. "If that's true," he replied, "the oil
people certainly don't need *my* vote." He refused to commit himself
one way or the other and was denied the Democratic leadership's
blessing.

Ways and Means is the strangest of all the House Committees—and
the hardest to understand [comments one reform-minded Democratic
congressman]. Judging by the voting records of its members on the floor
of the House, the liberals *ought* to have darn near a working majority.
But their public voting records and their "operating" records in the
Committee, behind closed doors, are two different things.

A labor-union lobbyist confirms this. He cites statistics compiled
by the AFL-CIO showing that twelve of the fifteen Democrats on
the Ways and Means vote "with labor" on major issues more than
two thirds of the time, eight of them more than nine tenths of the
time. Yet, he declaims angrily, few of them, in closed-door Committee sessions, will vote to tighten loopholes against the well-to-do,
as organized labor would like them to (and as consistency with their
usual voting pattern would lead one to expect).

### Strangled in the Citadel

While the pressure groups were active and vocal in opposition to
the 1963 Kennedy reforms, the general public was utterly silent. If
there was any proreform sentiment in the land, it was successfully
concealed from Congress. Perhaps one reason was the very tech-
nicality of the proposed reforms which, in turn, was due to the

complexity of the tax laws themselves. Consider this passage, chosen at random from the Internal Revenue Code:

> If the allowance of a deficiency dividend deduction results in an over-payment of personal holding company tax for any taxable year, credit or refund with respect to such overpayment shall be made as if on the date of the determination 2 years remained before the expiration of the period of limitation on the filing of claim for refund for the taxable year to which the overpayment relates.

Clearly, the tax code amply deserves its characterization, by tax attorney Louis Eisenstein, as "a remarkable essay in sustained obscurity," having "all the earmarks of a conspiracy in restraint of understanding." This complexity arms the experts and the insiders with unusual powers, and robs even the most vigilant congressman or newsman of his normal powers of scrutiny. What casual observer, for instance, would be able to spot a bill innocuously entitled, "A bill to amend Part III of Subchapter O of the Internal Revenue Code of 1954" as being a bill to provide substantial retroactive tax relief to the Hilton Hotel chain (and, potentially, nineteen other unsuccessful defendants in antitrust proceedings)?

So murky are tax measures that Congressman Patman of Texas has observed that they "are passed with the members not knowing exactly what they mean"—an argument used by some to defend the no-amendment rule governing House debate on a tax bill. Because of this rule, tax bills are quickly passed by the House and sent to the tender mercies of the Senate Finance Committee.

Senate Finance has been variously called "the citadel of conservatism" and the "happy hunting ground" for tax pressure groups. At times, such as the early 1950's, political liberals have had no representation on the Committee; at best, they have been an impotent and frustrated minority. This is not entirely accidental: the two current windmill tilters, Senators Albert Gore of Tennessee and Paul Douglas of Illinois, both say they had great difficulty gaining their Finance Committee posts. According to Robert Engler, in *The Politics of Oil* [Macmillan, 1961], at one point in 1955 a Committee vacancy thought sure to go to Douglas (a leading critic of the depletion allowance) was preempted by Majority Leader Lyndon Johnson, who later in the session handed on the seat to former Vice

President Alben Barkley, thus again stymieing Douglas. It was only on Barkley's death that Douglas finally won his Finance Committee seat.

Whereas Ways and Means has, of late, been headed by two stanchly reform-minded chairmen (Jere Cooper of Tennessee and Wilbur Mills of Arkansas), Senate Finance has for decades been dominated by a procession of men in whose hearts loophole-closing kindled no great flame: Reed Smoot (of Smoot-Hawley Tariff fame) of Utah; Pat Harrison of Mississippi; Walter F. George of Georgia; Eugene Millikin of Colorado; and Harry F. Byrd of Virginia.

Like all congressional committee chairmen, these men have possessed great power. For example, the fact that soft drinks were one of the few items that wholly escaped any excise tax during World War II, was not, according to knowing observers, wholly unrelated to the fact that the giant of the soft-drink industry, Coca-Cola, has its headquarters in Senator George's home state. . . .

Senate Finance sits as a court of appeals from the actions of the House. In theory, of course, the Treasury has an opportunity to appeal from Ways and Means' rejection of its tax-tightening proposals. But, as in the House hearings, the preponderance of pleas come from private-interest spokesmen, protesting such "reforms" as the House did enact (or seeking added tax concessions), and it is rare that a reform bill emerges from Senate Finance stronger, from Treasury's viewpoint, than when it passed the House.

Once Senate Finance has completed its work and a tax measure is placed before the full Senate for debate, the power of the Committee and its chairman are on full display. Understandably, the Senate regards the Finance Committee as its expert in tax matters, and by tradition the Committee chairman is the sole arbiter of the acceptability of outsiders' amendments. Consistency is not required in his screening. Senator Byrd, for example, once righteously rebuffed an effort by Vermont's Senator Ralph Flanders to bring tax relief to a particular Vermont citizen, on the ground that "this would establish a very dangerous precedent . . . attempting to pass a general law for one specific purpose"—while, on that same day, Chairman Byrd himself had shepherded through a measure tailor-made to bestow up to $4 million of tax relief on the estate of Mrs. Gerard Swope, wife of the former president of General Electric.

Frequently, loophole-closing amendments are either voted by the Senate or accepted by the chairman of the Finance Committee, only to perish shortly in the House-Senate conference committee. When, in 1959, a Senate repeal of the so-called dividend tax credit failed to survive the House-Senate conference, Senator Douglas was prompted to liken the fate of such loophole-closing actions "to the fate of the two young princes of England who . . . went into the Tower of London under very good promises but were strangled by Richard III and never emerged from the Tower."

### "We Get to Know Who Counts"

Not only do tax bills usually fail to contain the reforms asked by the Treasury; they frequently contain individually tailored provisions which, while mentioning no names, are so deftly drawn that their benefits are confined to a lone taxpayer. In 1951, the Senate Finance Committee tucked into a major tax measure a provision bestowing $2 million of tax relief on movie magnate Louis B. Mayer. And in 1956, the Senate appended to a House bill a provision reversing two court decisions and sparing an Oklahoma City contractor the unpleasantness of paying hundreds of thousands in back taxes and penalties.

Such special provisions are, by and large, the mark left on the tax laws by the Washington tax lobbyist. Typically, he is a lawyer, but he may be less sought after for his legal acumen than for his intimate knowledge of lawmaking and politics and, particularly, for his contacts on the Hill. Thus, he might well be an ex-senator or congressman or, perhaps, a former congressional staff aide. One former Treasury official tells of witnessing the Ways and Means Committee approve a tailor-made relief bill represented by a former Ways and Means staff member, on the ground that "we've got to do something to help out old ——."

The Washington lobbyist is likely to be generously rewarded for his efforts—his fee may run into the hundreds of thousands if his assigned mission is special relief legislation—but this is not astonishing in view of the considerable tax savings involved. The

$2 million provision for Louis B. Mayer is by no means unique;
one Washington lawyer matter-of-factly mentioned in a sidewalk
conversation that his success in changing a single date in one tax
measure meant a saving of $3 million for one client, and the mere
insertion of a parenthetical cross-reference in another statute
brought comparable savings to another.

Given their special power, the chairmen of Ways and Means
and Finance are clearly the most advantageous Hill contacts—
both for the lobbyist and his client. No one, perhaps, has equaled
the success, in this line, of Ellsworth C. Alvord, Mayer's personal
attorney, who was known to be on the most cordial terms with
Chairman George of the Finance Committee. . . .

The tax lobbyist is not likely to be found registered as such
under the lobbying law—Alvord, for example, did not register as
a representative of Mr. Mayer. (Many attorneys take the view
that the vaguely worded lobbying statute does not apply to the
particular activities in which they happen to engage.)

There is little talk in Washington of personal venality among
the senators and congressmen who sponsor special tax amendments,
but campaign contributions are another matter. One high-ranking
Senate Finance Committee member—asked by a reporter why he
uncharacteristically sponsored several pro-insurance-company
amendments—explained, in an unguarded moment, "This is the
way we finance our campaigns. Hell, I wish there was a tax bill
up every year."

The astute lobbyist seeks to minimize the Washington pressure
and maximize the "back-home" influences. Says one: "Over the
years, we get to know who counts with a congressman in his district." In 1963, for example, hometown insurance agents were effectively mobilized to protest to Ways and Means members the
proposed restrictions on tax-free group life insurance. One Committee member got an appeal on this subject from one of his most
trusted political supporters at home, and also—on behalf of the
oil-depletion allowance—from a friend and business associate who
was the local representative of a major oil company. The latter
acknowledged frankly that he was only calling at the behest of
company headquarters in the state capital.

To bolster congressional support for a bill making an exception for du Pont's court-ordered sale of all its General Motors stock, du Pont and GM each sent letters to their millions of stockholders urging them to write their congressmen and senators. The response was impressive.

Ordinarily, mail from constituents has little effect on a legislator's vote. But when it comes in torrents, it can be decisive—as it was in the case of the mail blitz credited with the 1962 defeat of tax withholding on dividends and interest. This blitz had its origins in private dining room Number 4 of the Palmer House in Chicago, on March 26, 1962, according to James McCartney of the Chicago *Daily News*. There, the "legislative subcommittee" of the United States Savings and Loan League—the trade association—resolved, after a four-hour debate, to organize a massive letter-writing campaign by the thirty million users of savings-and-loan institutions.

Four days later, a mailing went out to the League's 4,800 member institutions, with sample "Dear Saver" form letters to send to their customers. Treasury officials recall with bitterness what they feel was an erroneous implication in these mailings, that the proposed withholding plan involved a *new* tax, and not merely a means of collecting a tax that had been due all along. Reports McCartney:

Soon the deluge began to fall on the Capitol, first in letters by the handful, then by the box, then by the cartload, then by the carload. Before it was over [Senator] Paul Douglas had received 75,000 letters, Senator John Sherman Cooper got 60,000. Nobody in the Senate remembers anything quite like it.

At the time of the Palmer House meeting in Chicago, a Savings and Loan League expert estimated "we didn't have the votes in the Senate" to kill the withholding plan. But after the blitz, the vote in Senate Finance was 11 to 5 and in the Senate as a whole 66 to 20 against withholding.

Mail storms such as this operate in only one direction: they sometimes defeat but they never rescue a tax-tightening proposal; on the contrary, reform-minded congressmen report they get almost no proreform mail to spur them on—another of the cards that help to stack the deck.

## My Loophole Versus Yours

While the opponents of loophole-closing are single-minded and articulate, the forces of reform are divided and often mute.

> You would expect us labor guys to have gone all out to tighten up on expense-account high living [says one top-ranking AFL-CIO official]. But we had Actors Equity and the hotel and restaurant and bartenders' union on our necks telling us that an expense-account crackdown would ruin the theatres and the restaurant and hotel business. So while we went on record for the tighter rules, we couldn't mount an all-out campaign.

The voice of the Treasury can also be muffled. Congress makes no effort to conceal its distaste for outspoken Treasury reformers. During World War II, Randolph Paul, the dean of tax reform and then a top Treasury official, took to the speech circuit to defend the Roosevelt tax program. This incurred the displeasure of the chairman of Ways and Means and the speech-making came to a prompt halt. And President Kennedy's appointment of Stanley Surrey, Harvard law professor and apostle of tax reform, as top Treasury tax official, "spurred a vigorous effort by oil companies and other groups to block the appointment," the *Wall Street Journal* reported. Surrey was subjected to a merciless grilling by Senate Finance, and only an assurance by the Secretary of the Treasury, Douglas Dillon, that he, not Surrey, would decide tax policy, clinched Surrey's Senate confirmation.

Faced with a continuous uphill struggle, reform-minded legislators are likely to lose their zeal over the years. Minnesota's Senator Eugene McCarthy, who twice led the effort in the Senate to repeal the tax concession for corporate dividends, noted a severe attrition of his allies on the second go-round. His explanation: "A lot of Senators came to me and said, 'I took a lot of heat for my vote the last time—and anyway,' they said, 'it's futile.' "

The quest for tax reform isn't entirely futile. Many efforts to enact new loopholes are rebuffed; and Congress does, from time to time, abolish or constrict tax preferences—as, for example, in the stricter taxation of life-insurance companies in 1959 and of American businesses overseas in 1962. No one, moreover, should under-

estimate the staggering difficulty of the task confronting congressional tax-writers, for theirs is the toughest legislative job Congress
undertakes.

Nevertheless, over the years, the exceptions and preferences in
the tax laws have grown rather than diminished in number—largely, it would appear, because the general public either doesn't
understand about tax loopholes, or doesn't care about them, or both.

One member of Ways and Means—the most vocally reform-
minded of the twenty-five—thinks it's the latter.

The average American [he says, a bit regretfully] doesn't mind
other people having their own loopholes—he only cares about getting his.
So you shouldn't blame Congress or the committees about what the American people don't want. If we don't vote tax reform, it's simply because
there's no pressure for it.

## THE AGONY BEHIND THE SCENES [3]

In trying to adjust the flame under an "overheated" economy,
President Johnson has been less afraid of a little inflationary scorch
than of a sudden cooling that would congeal the whole brew.

The fear of doing too much—even while the experts were
clamoring for action—is said to have troubled the President
through three months of experimental fiddling and debate before
the Johnson recipe was sent to Congress this week.

Too many Presidents, Mr. Johnson kept saying, spoiled their
economic booms by inducing recession where they had meant only
to combat inflation.

Still another fear, as perceived by the President's closest aides,
was of the alarm that could spread through the financial community if the White House proposed bold steps—such as increases in
personal or corporate income taxes—only to have Congress reject
them.

### Inseparable Combination

If economic stability depends upon timely presidential intervention, Mr. Johnson contended, then it also depends upon a dem-

[3] From "The President's Tax Proposal: A Product of Fear and Study," by Max
Frankel, Washington correspondent. New York *Times*. p 76. S. 11, '66. © 1966 by
The New York Times Company. Reprinted by permission.

onstration that the President is in charge and can get the Congress to do his bidding.

Political and economic considerations thus became inseparable as Mr. Johnson spent the summer soliciting dozens of ideas for action.

The President tried out these ideas on scores of labor leaders, legislators and businessmen, at one point even asking Secretary of Defense Robert S. McNamara to pretend that he was again president of the Ford Motor Company and to react to a contemplated plan accordingly.

President Johnson studied briefs arguing for and against increasing income taxes, imposing wage and price controls and doing nothing before he settled, in late August, on a general plan of attack.

That plan finally evolved over Labor Day weekend into the message to Congress asking for the suspension of certain tax credits for all business investment in new machinery and construction and promising significant cuts in spending by the Administration.

### Interest Rate a Key

The hope behind these proposals is that a slower pace of private and public spending will ease the demand for loan capital, thus arresting the disturbing rise in interest rates on those loans.

By cooling off the country's most overactive industries—machine building and construction—the President also hopes to check rising prices and wages.

Mr. Johnson weighed all the arguments after provoking some of them by appointing devil's advocates. Then he is said to have become persuaded that though higher income taxes might best encourage the Federal Reserve Board to make loan capital less scarce, they would not bring down prices for at least several months, would not inhibit wage demands at all and would not retard industrial expansion soon enough.

Moreover, the leaders of Congress had no taste for raising income taxes in an election year. Through most of the summer they urged Mr. Johnson to try to get through the year without further legislative action. . . .

The more modest proposals finally submitted may yet encounter some bloody battles on Capitol Hill, the White House believes, but there have been enough cautious expressions of support to suggest final acceptance.

Mr. Johnson asked for a sixteen-month suspension of the provision that lets industry deduct from its tax bill 7 per cent of the cost of most machinery and equipment.

For the same period—September 1, 1966, through January 1, 1968—he wants to suspend the fast tax writeoffs, or accelerated depreciation, granted to builders and buyers of commercial structures.

### Special Pleas Expected

A number of industries—the railroads or airlines or big farms—are expected to plead for special consideration, arguing that their further rapid expansion is in the national interest.

In recognition of this plea, and to win more votes in Congress, the Administration seriously considered naming a special board that would grant continued tax benefits to selected investors.

But the idea was ultimately rejected as unfair and too cumbersome to execute. Mr. Johnson decided that a general suspension, without exceptions, was a program that could be portrayed not as a deprivation, but as a "bonus" to all industry to defer as much expansion as possible until 1968.

If this does not work, he is said to have concluded, there is ample time for further action in the next six months. But if, in his own metaphor, he applied the brakes too hard, there might not be another chance to avoid recession.

All ideas for fiscal action were assembled for serious study at the White House in June.

For almost a year before that, special committees of Cabinet officers and staff aides had fought what they regarded as a generally successful battle against inflation. Their tools were pressure and persuasion by the President, timely sales of Government stockpiles and more deliberate patterns of Government purchasing.

By holding down prices on aluminum, copper and steel, arguing down wage demands in some key industries and extracting

pledges from businessmen that they would defer about $1 billion
in new investments, the Administration thought until spring that
it could make do with a program of voluntary restraints.

Against the President's wishes, the Federal Reserve Board had
joined in the effort by raising the bank discount rate and otherwise
restricting the supply of money for loans, thus driving up interest
rates.

Though unwanted, this device had to be reckoned as among
the restraining influences, and some of the economists who preferred a rise in income taxes changed their advice to the White
House in the spring.

But then came signs that the tight money, while squeezing
small businessmen and homeowners out of the competition for
loans, was not cooling the boom in investment and commercial
building.

The backlog of unfilled orders for machinery and equipment,
up 27 per cent in the last year, was becoming even greater, toward
a total of 15 per cent in the last six months. The backlog of orders
for metal-cutting machine tools had grown to ten months, as
against six and a half months a year before.

### Signs of Inflation

Unemployment in the machine industry last spring [1966]
dropped to the amazingly low rate of 1.9 per cent and the average
work week went to forty-four hours, the longest in any industry.

The Bureau of Labor Statistics told the President that a handful of occupations accounted for two thirds of all hard-to-fill jobs
—machinists, machine shop workers, mechanics and repairmen,
welders, toolmakers, die sinkers and pattern and model makers.

The stock market was not recovering from its steady decline
since February. The consumer price index showed no signs of halt-
ing its steady climb and, statistically, 1966 became the most inflationary year since 1957.

Mr. Johnson called for "innumerable meetings" of a high-level
council composed of Mr. McNamara; Henry H. Fowler, Secretary of
the Treasury; John T. Connor, Secretary of Commerce; W. Willard
Wirtz, Secretary of Labor; Charles L. Schultze, Director of the

Budget Bureau; Gardner Ackley, chairman of the Council of Economic Advisers, and Joseph A. Califano, Jr., special assistant to the President. . . .

## Some Real Arguments

Sources . . . [in Washington] have refused to describe the nature of the arguments inside this group, except to say that some were real arguments while others were staged on different sides of the issues at the President's request.

Mr. Johnson solicited counterarguments from visitors, tossing the idea of an income tax increase to labor and of a suspension of tax credits to business and tossing both to his friends in the Congress. Every persuasive point was thrown back at his advisers for rebuttal.

By mid-July, this process was focused on some tax adjustment and not just firmer Administration action, and the President had a description of some part of the debate in his nighttime reading every evening.

In early August, Richard E. Neustadt, the dean of Harvard's School of Public Administration and author of *Presidential Power,* notified the White House that a whole group of experts in the Cambridge area was bubbling with ideas and debate.

Mr. Johnson told Mr. Neustadt to organize these ideas, and in mid-August the group sent word that it was ready.

The President sent Mr. McNamara, Mr. Fowler, Mr. Ackley and Mr. Califano to Cambridge on the night of August 22 and from the way they were sent they sensed that Mr. Johnson had now made up his mind to act.

Besides Mr. Neustadt they met with eight or nine specialists, including five Harvard economists—Otto Eckstein, John R. Meyer, John T. Dunlop, Carl Kaysen and Robert A. Solo—and the dean of the Massachusetts Institute of Technology, Howard W. Johnson.

Unanimously, the group recommended a cut in Federal spending and suspension of the 7 per cent tax credit for purchases of machinery. It was generally opposed to any attempt to impose wage or price controls.

Some of the experts are said to have urged an increase in corporate income taxes. Tax specialists among them hoped for an early abolition of all fast tax writeoffs—the accelerated depreciation benefit that Mr. Johnson would suspend only in the field of commercial construction.

Normal depreciation schedules allow a business to deduct from taxes a fixed part of the cost of an investment over a number of years. The principle of acceleration allows a much higher proportion of the cost to be deducted in the early years after purchase or construction.

The President heard the recommendations and now began talking in earnest with the congressional leaders of both parties, especially two influential Democratic committee chairmen, Representatives Wilbur D. Mills of House Ways and Means and George H. Mahon of House Appropriations.

Mr. Johnson also talked anew to businessmen, including Mr. McNamara in his Ford incarnation, who told him without exception that a suspension of the investment credit would lead them to defer from 30 to 60 per cent of their machine purchases.

Mr. Johnson kept telling them that the trick was to keep the boom going but to take the pressure off areas that were in trouble.

He showed them the signs of trouble in machine building, then added the reports on construction: the cost of building up 3.4 per cent in the second half of 1965 and 4.9 per cent the first half of 1966; all industrial contruction up 27 per cent over the previous year; the prices of cement and other materials running up and typical construction wages rising 6 to 8 per cent this year.

In the last week of August, Mr. Schultze's Budget Bureau was ordered to start looking for significant savings, both in the regular budget and in the amounts that Congress appropriated in excess of the President's requests.

By the start of the Labor Day weekend, those around the President believed that he had rejected raising income taxes but was still juggling variations in his program.

The juggling continued through the process of writing the message to Congress, starting last Sunday. On Monday portions of it were still being rejected by Mr. Johnson as unconvincing. Tuesday night it was set. Wednesday it was polished.

Having looked closely for about ten weeks, on Thursday the President leaped.

## WE'RE NOT READY FOR FINE ECONOMIC TUNING [4]

It is clear we have come a long way in our understanding and execution of both monetary and fiscal policy since the 1930's when poorly conceived and ill-timed policies contributed greatly to both the timing, magnitude and duration of the Great Depression. We now have the knowledge and political will to prevent malfunctioning of the economy at either the extreme of depression or hyperinflation. But public and political tolerance for economic malperformance has narrowed since the decade of the 1930's. There is, however, little evidence to indicate that our knowledge and political will have improved sufficiently to formulate and execute the kinds of "flexible" monetary-fiscal policies that will achieve and maintain the generally accepted domestic goals of stable growth at full employment with stable prices, to say nothing of achieving our international objective of eliminating the deficit in the balance of payments.

### Inherent Limitations of Activist Economic Policies

The hallmark of the new economics is that alert Government officials can consistently prescribe the proper public policies for maintaining economic stability. Despite the obvious political attraction of such a posture, there is little evidence that it can be successful. In fact, once the economy has achieved full employment of resources, thereby reducing the margin for error, an activist economic policy is very likely to be destabilizing.

There are many reasons for the shortcomings in economic policies and most are not due to imperfections in the marketplace but rather to imperfections in analysis and execution. There is a great temptation to characterize the private economy as a very unstable system constantly threatening to shift either into recession or depression on the one hand or into inflation on the other. According to this view, policymakers must be constantly alert and flexible, ready to fight either extreme by providing just the right amount of

[4] From "Destabilizing Policies in a Stable Economy," testimony presented before the Joint Economic Committee of the Congress of the United States, February 17, 1967, by Dr. Beryl W. Sprinkel, vice president and economist, Harris Trust and Savings Bank, Chicago, Ill. Text from release issued by the Financial and Economic Research Department of the bank. P.O. Box 755. Chicago 60690. '67. Reprinted by permission.

stimulus or restraint. A contrary view, which I believe is more nearly correct, is that the economy tends to be quite stable and frequent alteration in the degree of stimulus or restraint is more likely to destabilize the economy than achieve the avowed goal. The past one and one half years yields but another illustration of the hazards of frequent change in policies. This view is held not because of a belief that monetary-fiscal tools are impotent and therefore inconsequential, but rather the reverse. Monetary-fiscal changes have pervasive economic effects and frequent alterations are often so ill-timed that destabilization results. In addition to the obvious danger of insufficient political will, the lags in economic policymaking and execution almost assure us that serious mistakes will arise. The art of economic forecasting has improved but remains inadequate for the needs of activist policymakers.

There is first the recognition lag. This lag cost many months of time in late 1965 and early 1966 when the Administration refused to believe serious inflationary pressures were developing. There is the execution lag following recognition of the problem. Although for monetary policy this lag may be brief, it can be quite long for fiscal policy as witness the fact that it took over one and one half years to pass the 1964 tax cut. Finally, there is the impact lag which for both fiscal and monetary policy may be one to two quarters or longer. The private sector of the economy is now being depressed by the impact lag of the very tight monetary policy of 1966.

There are other complications which make success difficult. Monetary-fiscal authorities are not agreed as to the proper measure of policy changes and even if they were, it is difficult to gauge how much change is necessary to bring about the desired change in the economy. For example, monetary policy measurements proposed by various leading authorities include such diverse series as the change in bank credit, change in free reserves, change in interest rates, change in total reserves, and change in the money supply both broadly and narrowly defined. Fiscal policy measurements fare no better. For many years we were assured by congressional leaders and others that the fiscal impact should be measured by the administrative budget. The new economics taught us that only the full employment budget mattered. Some of us thought that the cash budget was the best measure, but recently the Council of Economic Advisers insisted that the national income budget is the proper budget for measuring fiscal impact. Unfortunately, the above proposed measures of monetary policy do not all yield the same answers and neither do fiscal measures. The basic point of the above remarks is that (1) we know much more about monetary-fiscal policies than we did during the Great Depression, but (2) our ignorance of detail concerning monetary-fiscal impacts is still so large that an attempt to sharply vary policies in order to "finely tune" the economy will almost certainly lead to serious errors, particularly when the margin for error is small.

## The Record—1960 to mid-1965

It is my view that both monetary and fiscal policies were unprecedentedly beneficial from 1961 through mid-1965 partly because the margin for error was great. Monetary-fiscal stimulus was provided and was clearly in order from 1960 through mid-1965 when substantial amounts of capital and labor resources were underutilized. There was considerable room for error for increased stimulation was unlikely to bring inflation but would hasten the employment of idle resources. Furthermore, monetary policy was quite stable from 1960 through mid-1965. During that period the money supply ... increased at a fairly stable 3 per cent annual rate. The only exception occurred during the first nine months of 1962 when monetary growth dropped sharply. Although the rate of rise in the economy was remarkably stable during most of the early expansion years, the economy faltered in late 1962 and threatened to go into a recession. Following the resumption in monetary growth in late 1962 the economy resumed its upward thrust.

Another additional major but, in my opinion, incorrect postulate of the new economics is that fiscal policy can be used in large measure as a substitute for monetary policy. Although fiscal policy received most of the plaudits for the 1961-1965 economic expansion, it should be noted that economic performance can be better explained by trends in monetary growth. Despite the fact that the 1964 tax lagged the initial proposal over one and one half years, the economy continued to record favorable growth records in response to an expansive monetary policy following the 1962 slowup. Furthermore, there was no demonstrable acceleration in the economy subsequent to the tax cut. Rather than looking on monetary-fiscal policies as substitutes, the evidence suggests they are more nearly complements with monetary policy providing the major spending motive force while the tax system establishes the structural incentives to encourage production, employment, saving, investment and growth. As pointed out later, the predominant influence of monetary policy as a spending inhibitor was again vividly illustrated during the past few months.

### Destabilization Since mid-1965

One could have dared hope that as the economy approached full employment of resources near mid-1965 a "flexible" monetary-fiscal policy would provide less stimulus. But alas, the stimulus increased! The Administration seriously underestimated the rising cost of the Vietnam war so that increased spending on defense and Great Society programs shifted the cash budget from a small surplus in the second quarter of 1965 to a sizable deficit. And, in fact, the cash budget probably underestimated the changing fiscal impact since the surge in Government orders, which initiated hiring and production, occurred well in advance of cash payments.

To compound the difficulty, monetary policy also became more expansive. In contrast to the approximate 3 per cent annual growth in the money supply from 1960 to April 1965, monetary growth doubled to 6.1 per cent from April 1965 to April 1966. Furthermore, measures of bank reserves and total bank credit reflected similar tendencies. In December 1965 when the Fed raised the discount rate amid great objections by the Administration, who argued that a tighter monetary policy was inappropriate, the money supply actually increased nearly 1 per cent, the largest monthly gain in nineteen years. As late as March 17, 1966, the majority report of . . . [the congressional Joint Economic Committee] condemned the discount rate increase because of lack of coordination with fiscal policy and also because it was apparently the Committee's view that a tighter monetary policy was inappropriate for the existing needs of the economy. Even though interest rates were tending upward due to sharp increases in demands for funds, monetary policy continued to fuel the flames of inflation by sharply augmenting the money supply.

We can properly ask why policies became more expansive just as the economy approached full employment of resources and inflation became a threat. The Administration clearly underestimated the inflation potential. To a considerable extent this was due to the sizable underestimation of Government spending. Congress consequently did not insist on a tax increase nor did it carefully prune nondefense spending. As the demand for credit accelerated, the Federal Reserve sharply augmented credit supplies, in the apparent but, in my opinion, mistaken belief that the rising trend in interest rates and declining free reserves meant monetary policy was becoming tighter. In fact, monetary policy became more expansive as the growth in total bank reserves, total bank credit and the money supply accelerated.

Several unfortunate consequences followed largely as a result of increased policy stimulus. Current GNP began to rise at a faster rate. Since resources were in tight supply, inflation became a serious problem for the first time during this economic expansion. For example, consumer prices rose 2.9 per cent in 1966 while wholesale prices increased 3.3 per cent compared to only 1.3 per cent and 0.4 per cent annual rate of increase from 1960 to mid-1965. As inflation anticipations accelerated and sales and order trends developed strength, there was increased impetus to borrow, and money and credit demands surged ahead. Despite the rapid infusion of reserves and new money, interest rates rose rapidly. The easy money policy in the year ending April 1966 engendered a tight money market by increasing inflationary fears and thereby stimulating credit demands. Although a change toward an easier monetary policy does in the short run tend to lower interest rates by increasing the supply of money relative to demand, a continued easy money policy tends to stimulate demand relative to supply, particularly when inflation develops. Therefore, an easier monetary policy resulted in higher rates. The truth of this concept is borne out not only by our recent history but also by modern history of most European countries which have had high rates of monetary growth accompanied by inflation and high and rising interest rates.

In early May of last year monetary policy abruptly changed gears and the money supply declined at a 1.7 per cent annual rate for the following seven months. Not only was the long-run impact of an easy money policy continuing to stimulate demand for money, but the sharp shift toward a tighter policy in the short run compounded pressure toward higher interest rates which peaked in August.

Furthermore, during the spring and early summer anticipatory borrowing began to develop as private borrowers became concerned that if they delayed making loan arrangements, credit might not be available. Federal Reserve officials accelerated this trend by refusing to raise CD [certificate of deposit] ceiling rates in line with rising market rates as had become the custom. In fact, the rate that commercial banks were allowed to pay on consumer-type deposits was cut from 5.5 per cent to 5 per cent. Therefore, banks were threatened with deposit liquidation and the necessity to severely reduce asset expansion. To compound the difficulties Federal Reserve officials made clear that they regarded bank loans to business as the major inflationary culprit. It was repeatedly stressed by Federal Reserve officials that banks must restrict loans to business or run the danger of not being able to borrow at the discount window. The move by Federal Reserve officials to blame excessive bank loans to business as the cause of inflation was analagous to the tendency of the Council of Economic Advisers to blame labor and business leaders for the same difficulty as they broke the economically unsound wage-price guidelines. Both actions reflected increasing tendencies to substitute administrative actions for market forces under the apparent but, in my opinion, mistaken conviction that the free market would not protect the public welfare. Although it is always tempting to blame nebulous private markets, excessively expansionary monetary-fiscal policies were clearly the cause of recent inflationary pressures.

Considering the unprecedented pressures placed on the money market last summer, brought about mainly by activist and inept financial policies, it should not be surprising that a near monetary crisis developed. It is a tribute to the efficiency of a hobbled money market that it was avoided.

Following the near monetary crisis in August interest rates receded significantly. Just as an excessively easy money policy stimulates the economy and the demand for funds, a policy of monetary restraint eventually has the opposite effect. Demand for credit began to abate by fall 1966 and finally in December the money supply rose slightly. In late December the Federal Reserve rescinded the September letter which requested banks to restrict business loans. Although free reserves continue to improve as interest rates decline, there has been little monetary expansion even up to the present despite the obvious weakness in the economy. To compound the difficulty, on September 8, 1966, the President asked Congress to suspend until January 1, 1968, the 7 per cent investment credit. Of all fiscal tools available, this one was probably the most cumbersome since its major effect could not be felt until well into 1967 when it was not clear that restraint would be needed. This change in signals has, however, already been very upsetting to some industries. For example, the American Railway Car Institute recently surveyed its members and based upon replies received estimated that only 10,028 railroad cars would be ordered in 1967. Since it is believed that 7,580 of these cars will be built in the railroads' own shops, no more than 2,448 will be ordered from outside carbuilders. In the last three years orders of railroad cars from independent builders were 1966—70,168; 1965—60,600; and 1964—40,518. According to the American Railway Car Institute, "It has now become clear that the suspension of the investment credit has dealt a staggering blow to the railroad carbuilders and their suppliers." The cost of this fiscal experiment will be measured in the loss of thousands of jobs and millions of dollars income. . . .

How can policymakers use their limited tested knowledge and demonstrated technical abilities to assure better economic performance? It is my view that policies should not be frequently adjusted for fine economic tuning. Despite laudable objectives, the results of such actions are likely to be destabilizing. Continued empirical research may eventually expand our knowledge to the point where "fine tuning" of the economy with flexible monetary-fiscal policies will be possible. In the meantime let us play the more cautious and prudent role of avoiding destabilizing action while providing moderate increases in total spending in line with the growth in the capacity of the economy to produce. A stable growth in the money supply of about 3 per cent per year similar to the 1960-April 1965 period accompanied by a Federal budget designed to attain approximate balance at full employment is probably the best we can do at present. . . . The gross mistakes in economic policymaking and execution of the recent past have convinced me that until our knowledge is substantially improved, an activist monetary-fiscal policy is quite likely to destabilize an inherently stable economy, especially once full employment has been achieved. In other words, a little knowledge can be a dangerous thing when ambitiously applied to economic affairs.

# VI. OUTLOOK FOR THE FUTURE

## EDITOR'S INTRODUCTION

What is the future for the new economics and for the use of taxation as a tool in maintaining a full employment economy in the United States? There is ample evidence that the basic principles work. But there is also evidence of formidable handicaps to their effective application.

This section deals with the current debate over the use of taxation as an economic tool and over the new economics in general. The first article takes a dim view of prospects. Because of tardiness in implementing the use of taxation as a tool in the recent past, it seems to the writer, a former editorial board member of the New York *Times*, that the method has lost ground.

In the article that follows, Walter W. Heller, former chairman of the President's Council of Economic Advisers, argues that the "time gap" problem could be remedied by granting the executive branch greater flexibility in taxation. The opposite view, reported in a news story, is taken by James Saxon, former currency comptroller, who proposes that monetary policy in addition to taxation be placed under greater congressional control.

The next selection—a series of comments by the head of a Swedish industrial association—goes beyond the immediate debate. The purpose of manipulating the tax rate and the other economic tools is to create an economy that provides ample employment for all. Sweden, he notes, has had full employment for many years. Thus the problems the United States now has have been faced before, and solved by Sweden.

The next article looks at the growing interdependence of economic planning in the international community. There is a rising awareness that one nation's economic health has a close bearing on the economy of its neighbor and this makes it all the more important to implement economic policies that lead to sound prosperity.

The selection that follows casts the current debate into perspective. Because of our command over economic tools like taxes and because of our knowledge of their effects, depressions are now obsolete. Thus even though bickering will continue about how best to use our economic arsenal the nation has already taken enormous forward strides in accepting fundamental concepts and changes that make the worst of our former economic woes impossible.

The final article, a review article by Edward Chase, examines the delicate balance that must be maintained between freedom and economic controls. Vesting more power in the central government may help to produce greater material prosperity but, Mr. Chase observes, citizens will have to be increasingly vigilant lest the price of the greater prosperity be diminished freedom for the individual.

## A LOST BATTLE [1]

The Johnson Administration . . . [has won] . . . a restoration of the investment tax credit for business spending but it is definitely losing its battle to introduce greater flexibility in its tax strategy.

There is a good deal to be said for raising and lowering taxes from time to time as a means of ironing out fluctuations in economic activity. . . . But this Administration plan for changing tax rates more often has suffered a setback as a result of its handling of the investment tax credit.

The investment credit has been used altogether too flexibly to suit Congress, which was pressed to suspend it last fall then asked to restore it this spring.

This quick reversal has soured both Republicans and Democrats, including Representative Wilbur D. Mills, the powerful chairman of the House Ways and Means Committee. In likening the Administration's tactics to changes in women's fashions, Mills insisted "we must not let ourselves be placed in the position of raising and lowering the hemline of taxation from season to season." . . .

[1] From "Fight for Flexibility in Tax Structure Appears to Be Lost," by M. J. Rossant, formerly a member of the New York *Times* editorial board, now director of the Twentieth Century Fund. New York *Times*. p 44. My. 18, 67. © 1967 by The New York Times Company. Reprinted by permission.

Yet, many private economists argue that what went wrong with the investment tax credit is that the Administration did not use it flexibly enough.

In their view, the idea of more flexible tax strategy has been needlessly jeopardized by the Administration's bad timing and maladroit handling of the tax credit.

They point out that the tax credit was originally proposed to spur corporate spending on new plant and equipment, which is a key to increased productivity and fast growth. But since capital spending tends to be extremely volatile, increasing when profits rise and declining when profits are squeezed, the incentive was supposed to be withdrawn whenever business threatened to spend too much.

But this plan to use the tax credit as a brake as well as a stimulus was not really put to the test. Although the credit was passed late in 1962, the Administration sat on its hands all during 1964, 1965 and most of 1966, when spending for new plant and equipment was rising at an average of 15 per cent a year.

Such a pace, which resulted in an enormous increase in the productive capacity of American industry, could not be sustained. But the Administration did not really make a move to temper it until last September [1966], just about when the squeeze on profits was first making itself felt.

While corporate spending might have leveled off in any event, there is no doubt that the suspension of the tax credit had an immediate effect on corporate plans. It was the right move at the wrong time.

Economists think that the Administration has now got its timing right. The incentive to invest is being put back just when spending seems poised for a fall.

Nevertheless, its economic impact is uncertain. Some companies may decide to speed up their spending plans, but with demand and profits declining, others will hold back for a while.

Private surveys suggest that spending on new plant and equipment will increase by about 5 per cent this year, which would not provide much of a tonic to the over-all economy but also would not be a depressant. However, failure to restore the credit might have triggered a serious decline.

The real trouble, though, is political. The Administration will have a hard time convincing Congress to suspend the investment tax credit when and if corporate spending rises too fast. And in view of its record, it will have an even harder time getting support for raising—or lowering—the hemline of individual and corporate taxes.

## A PLEA FOR MORE FLEXIBILITY [2]

[On the question of] . . . restraint in today's high-pressure economy . . . [it is clear] that our foot has to stay on the fiscal-monetary brake. . . . We should make some use of monetary policy in this connection without raising interest rates to the point where excessive pressure is put on savings and loan companies and other savings institutions.

Further monetary tightening must reckon with the constraints imposed not only by the position of the savings institutions but by growing international economic interdependence. Interest rates may not come down as readily in the post-Vietnam period as they have in the past. Dropping them faster at home than they drop abroad would run risks of substantial monetary outflows. Ways may be found of easing these constraints. But the course of prudence would seem to be to rely mainly on fiscal policy for such further restraint as we may need. . . .

My fiscal weapon of choice would be temporary income tax increases rather than expenditure cutbacks. The reasons are simple:

> Our weapon of choice for economic stimulus was $20 billion of tax cuts; the matching action today would be temporarily to "take back" $5 billion or $6 billion a year, i.e., cut private spending rather than Government civilian spending.

> Federal spending, as already noted, has shrunk as a percentage of GNP.

> Cutting Great Society programs would, in effect, finance the war in Vietnam and fight inflation at the expense of the poor.

[2] From "Adjusting the 'New Economics' to High-Pressure Prosperity," paper read by Walter W. Heller, former chairman of the President's Council of Economic Advisers, before a Committee for Economic Development symposium, Los Angeles, May 1966. In *Managing a Full Employment Economy.* Copyright © Committee for Economic Development 1966. 711 Fifth Ave. New York, N.Y. 10022. p 19-21. Reprinted by permission.

Taxes are much more quickly reversible. A temporary, highly visible, surtax could be—and, I believe, would be—removed very quickly to act as an economic stimulant after Vietnam.

Unlike Britain and Canada with their parliamentary system, we have no system of instantaneous—or nearly so—tax changes once the heads of government have made a decision. We should make every effort to shorten the period between fiscal decision and fiscal action, whether by streamlined congressional procedures, carefully hedged standby powers for the President, or other devices.

In today's situation, our contingency might well take—perhaps it is getting to the point where I ought to say "might well have taken"—the form of a contingent tax increase worked out jointly by the Administration and Congress, ready to be put through quickly by joint resolution upon presidential decision. I recognize both political and parliamentary difficulties. But I also recognize economic necessity. If a temporary tax package were preprocessed— if, in effect, we got the "Ready, aim" phase out of the way ahead of time—the Commander-in-Chief could say "Fire!" and have the tax gun go off with only a minimum delay. The prospect of a delayed reaction is itself a barrier to the right decision under our present system. Lowering that barrier would make fiscal policy not only more timely but more correct, both when more stimulus is needed, as in 1963, and when more restraint is needed, as in 1966.

In these remarks . . . I have talked primarily about Government economic policy. . . . But I would like to close by quoting the eloquent words Gardner Ackley used last fall on the interplay between private and public forces in our economy:

Our basic confidence must rest, as it always has, in the conviction that a free and competitive economy and an open and democratic society not only provide the basic human satisfactions that all men have always sought, but provide, as well, the most powerful engine for progress that mankind has yet devised. Government can and must clear away obstacles, reduce frictions, prevent abuses, and help steer the economy between the shoals of stagnation and the whirlpools of inflation. But the basic energizing force continues to be the strength, the will, and the imagination of free men.

## CONGRESS AND THE FEDERAL RESERVE BOARD [3]

James J. Saxon, who used to feud with the Federal Reserve Board on specific cases, scathingly attacked it on broad philosophic grounds as a menace to a democratic society.

Formerly the chief supervisor of national banks as Currency Comptroller in the Kennedy and Johnson Administrations, Mr. Saxon is co-chairman of the American Fletcher National Bank in Indianapolis. As a national bank, American Fletcher is automatically a Federal Reserve System member.

Arguing that the Board should be brought under closer political control, Mr. Saxon said its "claim to independence may have had some merit in the days in which the Federal Reserve sought no deliberate role in the making of vital social and economic choices." But, he said, "if it seeks to become a central planning board instead of a central bank, it is time that it should be brought under the purview of the elected representatives of the people" so its proposals and reasoning can be exposed to public view before it takes actions.

Mr. Saxon's remarks were made at the annual forecasting conference of the University of Illinois at Chicago.

A Federal Reserve Board spokesman said the board wouldn't have any comment on Mr. Saxon's speech.

"In a democratic society there are particular dangers in lodging broad regulatory powers with the central bank," Mr. Saxon said, accusing central bankers throughout the world of having "for centuries sedulously cultivated the view that monetary affairs have a mystique and an obscurity that calls almost for blind faith." Because of their "guise of benevolent conservatism," he said, "many a destructive policy may long escape notice or criticism."

Particularly with its present members, Mr. Saxon said, the seven-man Federal Reserve Board has got away from the original idea of simply providing enough money to permit economic growth and has "embarked on programs designed to promote or restrict the flow of credit to particular uses in the economy." It temporarily made an "ill-conceived and hazardous excursion" into trying to

[3] From "More Political Control Over Reserve Board Is Urged by Saxon, Citing Its Planning Role." *Wall Street Journal.* p 2. Je. 16, '67. Reprinted by permission.

pressure banks into limiting their loans to business customers last year, he said, and "still persists in its manipulation of the interest rate structure for the purpose of improving the competitive position of the savings and loan associations and stimulating the housing industry."

The Board's ambitions aren't solely domestic, Mr. Saxon contended, saying that "merely because it has to deal with other central banks," the Board "seems to regard itself as the ultimate arbiter of all our international financial affairs, both private and governmental."

The "most disturbing aspect" of these developments, Mr. Saxon charged, is "the insistence of the Federal Reserve that it should be allowed to exercise these powers independently, and in secret—powers which may be used, or abused, to favor or penalize one or another industry or segment of the economy, and thus seriously jeopardize the effective functioning of private enterprise in the public interest." The country must not allow the values of private enterprise, Mr. Saxon concluded, "to be subverted or compromised through incursions of Government sheltered from the cleansing effects of the democratic process."

## PROBLEMS OF A FULL-EMPLOYMENT ECONOMY [4]

This year [1966] the United States celebrates the twentieth birthday of the act which states that it is the responsibility of Government to create and maintain full employment. The celebration is congenial. It takes the form of the American economy approaching full employment. In Sweden we have no special employment act. But, nevertheless, we also are soon going to celebrate something—namely, the twentieth birthday of full employment.

As we have heard here, the soon-to-be-born full employment is already causing a lot of trouble. You are asking anxious questions. What will such a child do in the future? Will a full employment

[4] From comments by Axel Iveroth, Director General of the Federation of Swedish Industries, before a Committee for Economic Development symposium, Los Angeles, May 1966. In *Managing a Full Employment Economy*. Copyright © Committee for Economic Development 1966. 711 Fifth Ave. New York, N.Y. 10022. p 55-60. Reprinted by permission.

economy ever grow up and behave decently? What can we learn from other countries?

Having lived such a long time with full employment in Sweden, I have been asked to say a few words about the Swedish economy with special regard to wage and price policy problems. I don't want to make you unhappy about the future. My main theme, however, will be that a full employment economy may have not only a childhood, but, sorry to say, even a teenage period.

Let me first remind you of some basic characteristics of the Swedish economy. Sweden is a small country. The area is somewhat larger than California but the population is only that of Greater Los Angeles, which means less than eight million people. As most small industrialized countries, Sweden is much dependent on foreign trade. Almost a quarter of the national product is exported. That means two things for the economic policymakers of Sweden. First, they have fewer degrees of freedom in the choice of actions than they would otherwise have. Second, the Swedish economy is heavily influenced by what is going on in other countries.

The Swedish labor unions are mostly formed on an industrial and not on a craft basis. Accordingly there are very few disturbances caused by rivalry between unions. The manual workers' union has joined a top organization, the Confederation of Trade Unions, which has a much stronger grip on its members than the American counterpart, AFL-CIO. Salaried employees in Sweden are organized in unions of their own, having a special top organization.

On the employers' side the major dominating organization, the Swedish Employers' Confederation, has been given great authority to speak and act on behalf of its members.

A fundamental characteristic of the Swedish system of wage determination is that the labor market is only to a very small degree subject to state regulations. Wages and other conditions of employment are supposed to be determined through collective bargaining between the national federations of the Employers' Confederation and the national unions of the Confederation of Trade Unions. There is no compulsory arbitration in disputes of interest, except concerning the interpretation of valid collective agreements.

An interesting postwar development is the effort of unions and management (the parties on the labor market) to coordinate the wage negotiations through central framework agreements. During the 1950's and up to the present day there has been a switch from union-level bargaining to bargaining between the top organizations. The object of such central negotiations is to fix a margin for wage adjustments which is then put at the disposal of the unions for allotment among the various categories of workers. The idea behind this is that centralized bargaining is in the interest of the national economy. Rivalry among various unions in their efforts to get as big a slice as possible of the available "wage cake" for their own group has been said to be all too liable to spark off inflation.

The trend towards centralized bargaining has, of course, met a lot of opposition from those unions who have regarded it a sacrifice. At this point I will remind you of the fact that since the end of the war Sweden has had a Social-Democratic government. The connections between the trade unions and the Social-Democratic Party are many and cordial. Therefore, the trade unions in Sweden are not very inclined to challenge the official stabilization policy. The negative side of this, however, is that the government is afraid of challenging the trade unions.

During the last decade wages have risen about 8 per cent a year. Concurrently, consumer prices have annually risen 3.5 to 4 per cent. We have got so used to this that in most people's minds we simply have no special inflation. Our politicians start to worry about inflation when the prospects of annual price increases are higher than 5 per cent. There are, however, more and more observers who think—just as I do—that even in this field Sweden has to be more Americanized.

Only half of the total wage increases, however, are due to contractual increases. The rest, what we call wage drift, occurs at the company level over and above the contractual increases.

The growth of the national product has been satisfactory; between 1960 and 1965 real gross national product rose by 4.9-5.1 per cent a year. Astonishingly enough, Sweden has been able to register a more or less parallel development of the import and export curves during the last fifteen years. This has led to rather stable currency reserves.

The official attitude has been that there obviously is a fundamental conflict between a stable price level and full employment. The government has deliberately given full employment priority as the most important goal of economic policy. So far this attitude has not violated the other main goals, namely a steady and high growth rate of the gross national product and balance on the current external account. There are, however, indications that the imbalance in the domestic economy is leading to a continuing large deficit in the current external balance. Given the trend towards more stable price developments in the other countries, a continuation of the present cost increases in Sweden are likely to lead to difficulties.

The question then arises: What can be done to solve the crisis? This is not only a short-term problem. For the next several years there will be strained conditions. A newly published long-term survey has revealed that, in the years ahead, there will be a significant gap between demand for labor and the estimated growth in the labor force.

What is needed, first of all, is a policy aimed at restricting the growth of domestic demand in order to keep it within the limits set by the growth of capacity. Before making any comments about what has to be done, I will admit that in certain areas the government has acted with imagination and determination. In order to make the labor force as effective as possible Sweden is building an extensive machinery for the retraining and shifting of the unemployed.

Another innovation is Sweden's system of investment funds. The principle is very simple. Firms are stimulated through tax exemptions to set aside means for an investment fund of which 46 per cent is to be set aside in an account with the National Bank. The latter measure is taken in order to prevent this tax exemption from having liquidity-increasing effects on the part of the enterprises. At any weakening of the market, these funds can then be released for investment. . . . Otherwise, the Swedish arsenal is limited when it comes to avoiding excessive pressure on the economy. Because of a number of factors, Sweden's financial policy has become extremely fettered. On the income side of the budget she has reached a point where there is a very marked resistance against tax increases. Besides, it has become evident that the wage-earners in the fully organized Swedish labor market have succeeded rather quickly in gaining compensation for tax increases. On the expenditure side, public consumption expenditure has been kept at a very high level through long-term measures.

Although there is a lot of discussion about the necessity for restraint with public expenditures, the political possibilities of limiting them have proved to be slight, especially in view of the fact that, within the next two years, we are going to have two important elections. However, the awareness that present policies mean a tight mortgaging of our future resources has lately spread considerably, partly as a result of the break last year in foreign trade developments. Therefore, possibilities should exist for reducing our ambitions as regards public expenditures to a more realistic level.

I do not mean that we necessarily have to cancel welfare programs already agreed upon. What is badly needed is better coordination between resources and ambitions. The start of programs should be temporarily postponed, and later, when the time comes, they should be put into effect more gradually than so far has been the case. Note, I am not urging an end to welfare programs—only a moratorium.

As you all know, one general weakness with fiscal policy is the time-lags that are inevitably involved. It takes time until the statistics show that something is going on which requires action. Then the matter has to be discussed and investigated; just as is the case with your inflation. Then comes the slow parliamentary decision process. Then comes the introduction of the measures agreed upon. Until the results at last are registered—if at all—years may have gone by, and a completely different situation may then exist. I am of the opinion that there are great possibilities for making fiscal policy more flexible without giving the government *carte blanche*. For example, one way is to let the state—as the big companies do—operate with a set of budgets covering different periods and not only just one year. Other things being equal, this would mean more flexible timing.

Whereas Sweden's financial policy has been weak, her monetary policy has been all the more severe. It has, however, not been effective enough, as only a very limited part of the national product can be influenced through monetary measures. Furthermore, Sweden's relations to other countries put definite limits on her possibilities in this field.

There is always a temptation to become more protectionist when there are problems with the balance of payments. I am glad to say, however, that in Sweden the government, the trade unions, and the business community all agree upon the virtues of free trade. And as far as Sweden is concerned I have great hopes that this attitude will survive and guide our behavior in the coming, troublesome years.

## INTERNATIONAL IMPLICATIONS [5]

First, there has been a heightening of economic and social aspirations throughout the world. In the highly developed countries, this is directly evident from the priority which is given in national economic policy to the achievement and maintenance of "full employment" (along with continuing adequate gains in productivity). Partly because of their improved and generally successful record of economic management in the postwar period, the major industrial countries no longer consider the vicissitudes of the business cycle, and the threat of protracted periods of high unemployment, as being beyond the control of economic policymakers. In the less developed countries, where the concept of full employment is not clear-cut, this heightening of aspirations takes the form of emphasis upon a maximum rate of economic growth and upon rapid economic development. The desire of all countries—large and small, in widely differing stages of development—to achieve a continuous improve-

[5] From paper, "International Aspects of the Full Employment Economy," by Pierre-Paul Schweitzer, managing director of the International Monetary Fund, before a Committee for Economic Development symposium, Los Angeles, May 1966. In *Managing a Full Employment Economy.* Copyright © Committee for Economic Development 1966. 711 Fifth Ave. New York, N.Y. 10022. p 47-9. Reprinted by permission.

ment in the living standards of their populations is one of the most potent forces in the modern economic world.

Along with this universal desire for improving living standards, there has developed an increased awareness of the importance of financial stability, both domestic and external. Indeed, the high priority that is attached to economic growth and development has contributed to the concern about financial stability by aggravating the problem of maintaining it. Among the industrial countries there is widespread understanding that inflation, apart from its social inequities, sooner or later impairs the functioning of the domestic economy and causes balance-of-payments difficulties. It is realized that such difficulties complicate the task of managing the domestic economy and, if persistent or serious, may require the imposition of measures at least temporarily restrictive of economic growth. Among the less developed countries, it is true that a number of them have deep-rooted problems of financial imbalance arising from the attempt to promote development at a faster rate than permitted by domestic savings and the availability of foreign aid and capital. But in virtually all parts of the world it is now accepted that inflation is not the path to economic growth and to an equitable distribution of the benefits of such growth. Also encouraging is the increasing realization, as a lesson of experience, that when a financial imbalance is permitted to become progressively worse the eventual adjustment will be painful and disruptive.

Because of the heightening of economic and social aspirations and the increased emphasis being given to financial stability, countries throughout the world have multiple objectives in the formulation of current economic policy: a satisfactory rate of economic growth, high employment, a reasonable degree of price stability, and balance-of-payments equilibrium. For many countries, the framework of policy also includes the objectives of maintaining or achieving exchange stability and liberal trade and payments arrangements. Experience has demonstrated that only very seldom does it happen that all objectives are met simultaneously over any extended period. The instruments of economic policy invariably have limitations, in part reflecting institutional and political factors. Also, economic forecasting is inherently difficult because of ever-changing developments at home and abroad. Countries must thus engage in a continuous appraisal and adaptation of their economic policies, and the necessity from time to time of changing the relative priority of objectives or even making a choice among them is a universal experience.

Furthermore, the setting of economic policy formation, particularly in the major industrial countries, has been profoundly affected in recent years by the greater international integration of national economies. This has resulted primarily from the easing of restrictions on trade and from the movement of European countries in 1959 to external convertibility of their currencies. The enhanced freedom of goods and private capital to flow across national boundaries has brought new situations and problems, together with an understanding that policies of the major countries should be framed with an awareness of their impact on other countries and should not be inconsistent with the steady expansion of world trade. This growing recognition of the indivisibility of the world economy—of the interdependence of its parts—has led to an unprecedented advance in international financial cooperation. Many examples of this could be cited. But my main point here is simply that the development of a greater "international consciousness" over the past half-dozen years or so has added a new and important dimension to economic policymaking in the main industrial countries.

[Just how deeply interrelated the world's national economies are was dramatically demonstrated November 18, 1967, when the Labour government of Prime Minister Harold Wilson devalued Britain's currency by 14.3 per cent. Overnight, the British pound became worth $2.40 in United States currency instead of the $2.80 it had been before.

Within days other major nations rushed $3 billion in loans to Britain to "support" the devalued pound. In short, Britain could use the loan to pay off any demands made by countries to whom money was owed. In addition, three other nations—Denmark, Ireland, and Israel—almost immediately devalued *their* currency in the wake of Britain's move. They felt they had to in order to stay competitive. After the devaluation Britain's goods, relative to those countries that did not devalue their currencies, were 14.3 per cent cheaper. Hence, to continue to compete in Britain and in those countries in which their goods compete with British products, these nations felt they also had to devalue their currencies.

The main economic condition that prompted the devaluation is that Britain, as a nation, had consistently bought more abroad than she sold. Just as with any individual who spends more than he earns, there finally came a point when Britain had to correct the imbalance. Devaluation, a drastic, unpleasant step, seemed to be the answer.

But how did Britain get into such a bind? One major reason is that economic policies at home failed. The Wilson government put through a year-long austerity program that included sharply higher taxes and interest rates. The aim was to curb buying of foreign goods and to increase exports. The results, unfortunately, were minimal and, when the restrictions were eased, the trade gap widened even further. Finally, with the devaluation of the pound, the impact of the failure of these policies spread beyond Britain's shores to have a distressing impact on the economies of other nations.—Ed.]

## TO SOME EXTENT, THE BATTLE IS WON [6]

[In the United States] in the twenty-year period since World War II there has not been anything closely resembling a depression, in the classic sense of that term—mass unemployment, idle factories and collapsing farm prices. There have been five recessions—statistically defined as periods of about a year when production was heading down instead of up and unemployment rose—but all have been mild and brief. An entire generation has grown up without the grim knowledge of what a depression can be like. Though there might be some quarrel about dates and definitions, it is probably safe to say that this is the first generation since the industrial revolution began 175 years ago never to experience a depression. . . .

This remarkable performance is by no means confined to the United States. Quite the contrary. The industrial nations of West-

[6] From article, "We Are Depression (But Not Recession) Proof," by Edwin L. Dale, Jr., New York *Times* correspondent specializing in economic affairs. New York *Times Magazine*. p 36+. Ap. 4, '65. © 1965 by The New York Times Company. Reprinted by permission.

ern Europe have done even better. While experience differs somewhat from country to country—Britain, for example, has not performed as well as West Germany or Sweden—some countries have not had even a recession for ten years. What recessions there have been in individual countries . . . have on the whole been even milder than those suffered by the United States. And again, there has not been the slightest hint of a depression in the classic sense. Good business and high employment have consistently been the rule.

This sort of record in the industrial world naturally raises some interesting questions. Perhaps the analogy with medicine is the most apt. We have learned virtually to wipe out polio and tuberculosis. In the same scientific sense, have we fully mastered the prevention and cure of depressions? And, as medicine goes after cancer, can governments so refine their knowledge and their actions as to abolish even recessions as well?

While economics is not nearly as exact a science as medicine, and never can be, the scientific analogy is still proper. We are performing better economically because we know more—far more—than was known a generation ago. True, public acceptance, or even understanding, of the new theories and tactics in economic management is by no means complete; while people leap to new cures in medicine, they look with suspicion on new techniques of government finance. But public acceptance is gaining all the time, and meanwhile governments are boldly pursuing the new methods.

That returns us, then, to the first question: Are we depression-proof? And if so, what has made us so?

I believe it can be said with safety that we *are* depression-proof. Some men, while agreeing with this general proposition, might argue that the one eventuality we could not control—possibly resulting in another depression—would be a collapse of the international financial system, based on gold, which is currently under some strain. This certainly stands as a warning sign and as a cause for redoubled efforts, which are under way, to make sure the system does not collapse. But the basic statement stands: We are depression-proof.

There are two sets of factors that make us so. One category can be described as defensive reforms, nearly all of them enacted willy-nilly during the years of the last depression, in the 1930's. The second category is improved government knowledge of and weapons against the business cycle.

Everyone alive and prospering today owes an eternal debt of gratitude to the men of the New Deal who, often groping their way, built our basic defenses against depression. Most of the changes were in what can be called the financial area. Typically, all through history, depressions have been either started or made worse by crises in the field of money and finance, ranging from bank failures to collapses of the stock market.

Possibly the greatest single reform of the New Deal—though one of the least heralded—was bank-deposit insurance. A wave of bank failures, such as happened in 1932 and 1933, is now impossible. "Runs" on individual banks may still be possible, but they are so rare as to be all but extinct. Nationwide runs are gone forever, which is as significant a change in economics as the prevention of smallpox in medicine.

Another key set of reforms involved the stock market. It became regulated for the first time. Equally important, a limitation was imposed on stock market credit, thus ending the 1929 situation when a man could buy $1,000 worth of stocks by putting up $50 of his own money. Stock market declines—even steep declines—are by no means ruled out, as the "Kennedy break" in the spring of 1962 revealed. But the excesses of 1929 are ruled out. Individuals can still take a fearful beating in stocks, but it is most unlikely that the stock market will ever again lead the whole economy into the depths.

A third key New Deal reform—though one that is by no means an unmixed blessing—was farm-price supports. Collapses of farm incomes have been a classic cause or companion of depressions, and they are no longer possible. True, the price-support system has given us the headache of surpluses and large Government outlays on agriculture, but in the long view this seems a price worth paying.

Next in the list of defenses is the system of income support, headed by unemployment compensation. Here is a dazzlingly simple mechanism to check the spiraling effects of a downturn in production. Men laid off have some money to spend and so their buying does not dry up completely, as used to happen. Social Security and the various measures for Government relief of the needy are also income supports, working of course in both prosperity and downturn.

Somewhat more controversial, though still clearly an income support, is the combination of minimum wage laws and contractual wage agreements negotiated by labor unions, which were enormously strengthened in the New Deal years, These wage floors are regarded as a mixed blessing by some economists, but it will never again be possible for the entire wage structure of the economy to collapse, as could occur in depressions, with adverse consequences for total spending and hence production.

Finally, back in the financial area, there should be mentioned the complete break with gold domestically and a set of reforms enabling the Federal Reserve System better to control the nation's money suply. Although the young today might scarcely believe it, the United States money supply dropped by more than 50 per cent between 1929 and 1933—cause enough in itself for a depression.

So much for the basic defenses. They are so formidable that one can imagine the following hypothetical situation: A Government of our great-grandfathers, with none of the modern knowledge of economics and Government finance, would be in office tomorrow when a downturn in the economy began; because they knew no better they would take no conscious action to improve the situation; but the defenses would operate so well that the economy, after a recession, would soon pull out of the slump of its own accord. There would be no depression.

But in addition to the defenses against depression, we also have the bonus of improved knowledge and Government techniques as well. They center on the use of the Federal budget.

It seems almost incredible now, but both candidates in the presidential election of 1932 urged a balanced budget as essential to cure the depression. Their views were supported by the majority of economists at the time—though a then-obscure Englishman named John Maynard Keynes was arguing strenuously the opposite.

Fortunately President Roosevelt soon permitted the budget to move into deficit, which helped to bring a partial recovery from the depression, but he did so reluctantly. What is more, he committed what would be regarded now as the major blunder of raising taxes while the depression was still under way—to keep the budget deficit from growing, he thought.

Now, of course, we recognize budget deficits as positively beneficial in times of economic downturn. This was thanks largely to Keynes, who thought out the role of Government in sustaining total demand in the economy. If the Government spends more than it takes in through taxes, and borrows the difference, total spending in the economy is increased. More goods and services are produced, more men and women are put to work, more incomes are earned and eventually business turns up again.

The business and banking community in the United States now fully accepts "modern" fiscal policy in the case of depression. The change in thinking began with a remarkable statement shortly after the war by a group of moderate businessmen calling themselves the Committee for Economic Development; now it has gone so far that Barry Goldwater in the last campaign accepted the need for budget deficits in the case of a depression. The relatively conservative Eisenhower Administration came up with a $12 billion deficit during the recession of 1958 and the recession soon ended.

The same basic defenses and modern knowledge that have made us depression-proof exist in Europe. In a sense, European financial men tend to be even more conservative than their American counterparts, but they accept both the reforms in structure and the use of government deficits that have made full-scale depressions a thing of the past. Governments, of course, have no doubts about what is needed. And the results are there to be seen.

But because one of man's glories is his constant striving for perfection, ending depressions forever is not enough. Now comes the next question: Can we end even mild recessions as well? It is a question that cannot be answered categorically, but the subject is very much alive today.

First, some sort of definition of recession is necessary. Definitions may differ, but perhaps a fair one would go about like this:

The economy suffers a recession when industrial production trends downward for at least six months and unemployment rises during that period. This is a "tight" definition. Some experts would insist on more than six months as a test, but no matter. Our goal, after all, is a total cure. But it should be said that if we never again had a recession of more than six months, we would be pretty close to the total cure.

In considering whether recessions can be eliminated, one key point to be noted is something not widely realized in the United States. This is that, in our current situation, we are less able to "afford" recessions than we were.

The chief reason is our level of unemployment. Mainly because of an unusually rapid growth of the labor force resulting from the teen-age explosion, we still have [in 1965] more than 3.5 million unemployed despite a consistently strong performance of the economy and rapidly rising output. Last year the growth of the economy created 1.5 million new jobs—a net increase, allowing for jobs lost through mechanization—but unemployment was reduced by only 300,000. Our present unemployment rate of 5 per cent of the labor force is clearly too high, even though the jobless rate among adult men is down to its level of prosperous periods in the mid-1950's.

During the current expansion, which began in March 1961 and has been spurred by conscious Government action such as last year's big tax cut, we have slowly and painfully reduced unemployment from above 6 per cent to the current level of 5 per cent of the labor force. But we have to run very fast to gain at all. If there were a recession, the rate would jump very quickly back to 6 per cent and well above. The process of reduction would have to begin all over again.

A second reason mentioned by some observers for feeling that a recession now is more than ever undesirable—even if cured relatively soon—is that we would begin it with an already existing budget deficit. Moderate deficits have been consciously used by the present Administration to spur the pace of the expansion and reduce unemployment, and this has been increasingly accepted as sound policy. But a recession, both through its automatic effect on most Government receipts and some expenditures, and through whatever conscious Government measures were taken to check it, could balloon the deficit from the present level of around $5 billion to $15 billion or more. This might not bother many economists, but it could have a bad psychological effect on the general public, and the business community in particular. Whether this is a real problem or not, it is an added reason for hoping strongly that a recession can be avoided.

And so we come back to the question: Can it be avoided? Can the business cycle be abolished altogether?

Recessions, and in the old days depressions, have usually been brought on by what are termed "excesses" during the preceding period of prosperity. A classic case, and cause, is inventory accumulation.

Because of prospective shortages, or rising prices, or because of overoptimism as to future sales, businesses stock up with more goods—raw materials at the manufacturing level, finished goods at the wholesale and retail level—than they customarily keep in inventory. At some point, this process stops and reverses itself. Buying virtually ceases for a while—as every businessman knows from experience. Even the statistics—and ours are the best in the world—let him know only where the economy was last month and not what is happening today.

Thus he does not know whether inventory building is excessive, or even whether prices are rising; not knowing, he cannot make a sure decision whether to move toward restraint or expansion of total demand. And while the monetary authorities—the Federal Reserve—can move very quickly, the fiscal authorities cannot. The budget comes but once a year, and then the glacial processes of Congress take over.

The foregoing presents a pessimistic, or at best skeptical, picture of the Government's ability to prevent excesses, and hence to prevent recessions. But there is a happier side to the story, deriving from the current situation in the United States and the current policy thinking in the Government....

The Government is doing two things to ward off, or at least to check, recessions. First, it is making sure that, as long as excesses and particularly inflation do not develop, its current policy is expansionary. Both monetary and fiscal policy are now being used to expand demand, not to check it. This is safe, without inflation, as long as there are idle resources of men and plant. No longer does the Government aim to balance the budget just for the sake of balancing it; instead, if the state of the economy calls for more demand, the budget is purposely put into deficit. . . .

Second, the Government is seeking better methods for rapid action against recession if one should develop. The President has asked Congress to take a look at its procedures and work out a method of quick action on a temporary antirecession tax cut if the President should call for one. And in the Administration a search is under way for those forms of Government purchasing that could be rapidly expanded in a recession. While public works are not excluded, it has been found that they take too long to get under way, and so other areas of spending are being explored.

Thus it is quite likely that if another recession does develop, the Government will move against it with better and more rapid weapons. The objective, of course, would be to shorten the duration of the recession, at the expense of a temporarily enlarged budget deficit.

This, then, is the current state of affairs on the recession front. The President in his economic report said, somewhat cautiously, that recessions "are not inevitable." The chairman of the Council of Economic Advisers under President Eisenhower, Raymond J. Saulnier, told a congressional committee recently that, with proper Government and private policies, the present expansion could be kept going "indefinitely." But despite these expressions of genuinely felt optimism, few men are arguing that recessions will be, or can be, abolished forever.

Yet as long as things go on as they are going in the economy, no recession seems imminent. Our boom is not "running away" and creating excesses, at least not so far. And thus, even without any magic new cure—which does not exist—we may be escaping recessions simply by a combination of sensible policies and actions by both the Government and private business. The old devil business cycle is not dead, but it surely appears to be losing its grip.

## ECONOMICS AND FREEDOM [7]

Something unexpected is happening behind the headlines. A world is being changed by theory. This is exciting in itself. After all, Daniel Bell and his fellow sociologists certified for us in 1960 that the 1950's had witnessed the end of ideology. However, *theory,* apparently, is quite another matter. The implementation of Keynesian economic theory has quietly yet decisively changed the postwar Western world. It has virtually freed it from the devastations of the business cycle. But this accomplishment has strengthened the conviction among some that economic science has reached a level of sophistication whereby it can end other, more stubborn economic ills—at least once Vietnam is behind us. This article will deal with this new train of thought in a moment. First some background.

For the United States, today's belated acceptance of Keynesianism means at a minimum an end both to the kind of economic stagnation of the 1930's and to our deficient growth rates and attendant unemployment of the 1960's. The term Keynesianism or "neo-Keynesianism" has become loosely interchangeable with "the new economics." "The new economics" actually is journalese for the political economics featuring the tax cut practiced by the Kennedy-Johnson Administrations, notably under the aegis of Walter Heller. With its customary prescience, the *New Yorker* magazine recently carried a cartoon showing an urbane upper-middle-class wife commenting to her husband as they read the newspapers in a chic modern apartment, "I don't know a darn thing about Walter Heller. I just like to know he's there." He is no longer in the Council of Economic Advisers but he remains a powerful figure in national economics policy deliberations.

What must be understood about the new economics is that, besides being comforting, it is evolving. It is a changing complex of ideas that is triggering a new, higher level of political-economic discussion quite free from the ideological quarrels of yesteryear. Walter Heller himself makes this clear in his authoritative new book, *New Dimensions of Political Economy,* the 1966 Godkin

[7] Review article by Edward T. Chase, free-lance writer who has written extensively on urban planning, economics, and national resources. *Commonweal.* 85:254-6. D. 2, '66. Reprinted by permission.

lectures at Harvard. Several other notable books have come along recently that help to put contemporary economics into longer perspective. Robert Lekachman has given us *The Age of Keynes* (Random House), Andrew Shonfield *Modern Capitalism* (Oxford), and Robert Heilbroner *The Limits of American Capitalism* (Harper).

Lekachman demonstrates with the greatest lucidity how and why Keynes' notion of aggregate demand economics, necessitating the decisive intervention of the central government, came to prevail. Shonfield, in a remarkably cogent survey of the changing state of capitalism among Western nations, celebrates the growing sophistication with which planning now modifies the West's free economics. Heilbroner, more philosophical and speculative than Shonfield, first briefly recapitulates the recent changes in American capitalism and then raises disturbing questions about the future. He takes us decades beyond the considerations of the relentlessly pragmatic Walter Heller. With Shonfield, he poses some ultimate issues precipitated by the new economics: the problem of reconciling planning—aimed at controlling the irrationality of the market and masterminding the impact of new technology—with decentralization and political freedom. Or, to put it more specifically, he poses the problem of maintaining a tolerable degree of freedom of consent by the governed in a society where the elitism of "experts" is inevitable because of the ascendancy of science.

Thus, while the well-to-do lady in the *New Yorker* cartoon is rightly comforted by Walter Heller's achievements—all but the very poor have been the beneficiaries of the tax cut he directed and the resultant jump in the economic growth rate—one consequence of the success of the new economics is a sharpening of awareness of how much it hasn't accomplished, of what economics must still do in order to provide a tolerably just social order. Note the recent "Freedom Budget for All Americans" subscribed to by Robert Lekachman, Daniel Bell, Robert Heilbroner, Michael Harrington and John Kenneth Galbraith, among other policy formulators. It is aimed at eradicating poverty in a decade by spending $185 billions on domestic welfare programs, including a guaranteed income for the unemployable. For another instance, "the years of the economist" is what Galbraith dubbed the past quarter-century in his recent address at the Urban America symposium. Galbraith had in mind the national obsession of the 1950's and 1960's with using "the new economics" to up the economic growth rate so as to match Japan's and Western Europe's. But he went on to deplore this obsession because it has diverted concern, to a disastrous degree he claims, away from the *qualitative* aspect of our national life—in particular the need to upgrade our urban services, such as health care, housing and transportation.

The common factor in Galbraith's presentation and in the books by Lekachman, Shonfield, Heilbroner and even Heller is a new-fangled preoccupation with an old-fangled subject, the place of the market system. It is a preoccupation that in their books is in a context of thought and rhetoric that is of a different universe from the Socialist polemics of the 1930's. It is a dispassionate consideration of how the market has been and must be tamed. Of how the market has been aided (largely by Keynesianism) to work with a marvelous new efficiency. Of why the market's negative effects are so many and distressing. And what forces may eventually end the market's dominating position as the dynamic of the Western world's economies.

None would dispute that "the market" in the broadest sense represents much that has been precious to modern Western man since the end of feudalism. It has been the very foundation of individual entrepreneurship and the opportunity for self-fulfillment; for harnessing the tremendous forces of self-interest; for decentralization; for competition; for the freedom to choose one's work and for social mobility. It has been Adam Smith's magical tool for the automatic allocation of resources through a pricing mechanism whose sensitivity and precision make it the envy of totalitarian planners.

The reason it is hard for an American to appreciate how huge the market looms in our scheme of things is because it is so pervasive, so taken for granted. Bear in mind that the life energies of the majority of Americans, all those millions who toil within the business system, are absorbed in its workings. And, as Charles E. Lindbloom shows in the summer issue of *The Public Interest,* the market is being increasingly used in Russia and in other socialized economies.

## The Next Stage

What, then, disconcerts these non-Marxists, non-Socialist, non-totalitarian market-preoccupied economists? It is important to know if one is to understand the next stage in economic discourse. The answer is the paradox that the market, to which we are beholden for our treasures, by its very nature gravely complicates (1) our progressing to a more just society and (2) our ability to cope with the technological explosion. Hence, at the very moment of capitalism's triumphant harnessing of the market, the thrust of Western liberal economic thought in important quarters is to demonstrate the market's inherent inadequacies.

The paradox is the sharper for the fact that what is most valuable about the market on economic grounds, namely that its prices reflect with exquisite precision the ebb and flow of demand, is also its Achilles' heel. How come? Because the market is inoperative so far as reflecting social costs and benefits are concerned. This has misled Americans (to the horror of cultivated foreign observers) into assuming that such nonmarket costs and benefits do not count. Shonfield in *Modern Capitalism* makes the point well:

> Increasingly the realization is forced upon us that the market, which purports to be the reflection of the way in which people spontaneously value their individual wants and efforts, is a poor guide to the best means of satisfying the real wishes of consumers. That is because market prices generally fail to measure either social costs or benefits . . . unless the state actively intervenes, and on an increasing scale, to compel private enterprise to adapt its investment decisions to considerations such as these, the process of economic growth may positively impede the attainment of things that people most deeply want.

Another way in which to understand the limited role of a profit-inspired market system is to observe that nonprofit services, like mass transportation or health care for the indigent elderly, cannot generate effective market demand. Businessmen, however, more eager to minimize the Government's role in the social order than to concede their inability to provide the services, pretend otherwise. Hence we see the insurance industry fight off Medicare for a quarter of a century on the pretense they could "meet the demand."

There are more subtle tests than Medicare that reveal the danger of leaving public policy decisions up to the market. Take environmental pollution. In terms of the price market system, how can an economist gauge the true costs, say, of an elevated urban highway as contrasted with an underground transit line? For here the social ramifications are enormous and the market offers no help. And what of truly complex public policy questions that are bound up with technical matters requiring an understanding of nuclear physics, for example? It is apparent that we must have recourse to authoritative, expert counsel.

Heilbroner is at his most provocative here. He suggests that the market-oriented business mind will gradually give place, in our social order, to the mind of the scientist and technologist, who are hostile to irrationality and will want to invest a rationality into the social-political order akin to that in science. He writes of

the profound incompatibility between the new idea of the active use of science within society and the idea of capitalism as a social system. The conflict does not lie on the surface, in any clash between the immediate needs of science and those of capitalism. It lies in the ideas that ultimately inform both worlds. The world of science, as it is applied by society, is committed to the idea of man as one who shapes his collective destiny; the world of capitalism to an idea of man as one who permits his common social destination to take care of itself. . . . Before the activist philosophy of science as a social instrument, this inherent social passivity of capitalism becomes archaic and eventually intolerable. The "self-regulating" economy that is its highest social achievement stands condemned by its absence of a directing intelligence. . . .

Thus does Heilbroner anticipate science and technology undermining capitalism, with its market dependence, as earlier the market system superseded the feudal order. Some version of national planning, for example as practiced in France, one which uses social cost-benefit analysis, may be the first step toward the new order. But the rub is that it must be planning with government teeth of sorts, if it is to work.

As of now, public questions in the United States are settled on the basis of conflict, market competition, or to borrow a suggestive analogy from our legal system, through adversary relationships. Even when scientists vie for Government funds for research it is essentially a contest among contending pressure groups rather than an objective weighing of evidence, as Robert Oppenheimer recently stressed at Columbia University's celebrated Seminar on Technology and Social Change. In a word, our social system operates for the most part on the basis of adversary relations among a mélange of contending interests. In this way "the market," in the broadest sense of the term, becomes equated with "freedom." It stands for decentralization and the sovereignty of the individual consumer.

But does history show that this contention of diverse small groups insures freedom? A recent profound study of this question by the University of Chicago political scientist-historian, Grant McConnell, suggests otherwise. In his study, *Private Power and American Democracy* . . . [Knopf, 1966], he finds the American experience shows that the public interest has been best served in the main *not* in consequence of free competition among many small competing constituencies but, instead, when large constituencies have prevailed. McConnell thus favors nationally based constituencies like the presidency, the party system, the Federal Government.

Generally, McConnell writes, "the liberty of individuals is more secure in a large constituency than in a small and the larger the constituency the more probable is it that the group is committed to equality." The pluralist is under a delusion in believing "grass roots" and Government deference to private groups with concrete narrow ends somehow ameliorates the phenomenon of power. More often than not the public interest becomes lost in the contentions of private interest groups, which usually achieve their ends through the collaboration of administrative agencies (the FCC, the SEC, the ICC, the CAB, etc.).

This welcoming of centralized power is at once surprising and encouraging, to be sure. But it can hardly altogether dispose of one's basic anxiety that deference to an establishment dominated by a scientific-oriented elite will nonetheless place great strain upon us to devise political institutions and processes that ensure a government founded on the free consent of the governed. Rationality, yes, but the great challenge to the political economists of tomorrow is to see to it that we do not purchase it at the expense of liberty.

# BIBLIOGRAPHY

An asterisk (*) preceding a reference indicates that the article or a part of it has been reprinted in this book.

## BOOKS, PAMPHLETS, AND DOCUMENTS

Benoit, Emile. Europe at sixes and sevens: the Common Market, the Free Trade Association, and the United States. Columbia University Press. New York. '61.

Chamber of Commerce of the United States of America. Committee on Economic Policy. Goals of economic policy; report. The Chamber. Economic Research Department. Washington, D.C. '61.

Chamber of Commerce of the United States of America. Committee on Economic Policy. Promise of economic growth: prospects, costs, conditions; report. The Chamber. Washington, D.C. '59.

*Committee for Economic Development. Managing a full employment economy; a CED symposium held in Los Angeles, May 1966. The Committee. 711 Fifth Ave. New York 10022. '66.
    Reprinted in this book: Adjusting the "new economics" to high-pressure prosperity [address]. W. W. Heller. p 8-21; International aspects of the full employment economy [address]. P. P. Schweitzer. p 46-55; Discussion [from Swedish viewpoint]. Axel Iveroth. p 55-60.

Dennison, H. S. and others. Toward full employment. McGraw-Hill. New York. '38.

Doris, Lillian, ed. American way in taxation: internal revenue, 1862-1963. Prentice-Hall. Englewood Cliffs, N.J. '63.

Galbraith, J. K. Affluent society. Houghton. Boston. '58.
    Review. Fortune. 59:112-13+. Mr. '59.

Galbraith, J. K. Economic development. rev. ed. Harvard University Press. Cambridge, Mass. '64.

Gillman, J. M. Prosperity in crisis. Marzani & Munsell. New York. '65.

Groves, H. M. Financing government. 6th ed. Holt. New York. '64.

Heilbroner, R. L. Limits of American capitalism. Harper. New York. '66.

Heller, W. W. New dimensions of political economy. Harvard University Press. Cambridge, Mass. '66.

Hellerstein, J. R. Taxes, loopholes and morals. McGraw-Hill. New York. '63.

*Income, employment, and public policy: essays in honor of Alvin H. Hansen. Norton. New York. '48.
    Reprinted in this book: Burden of the national debt. A. P. Lerner. p 255-75.

Keynes, J. M. Economic consequences of the peace. Macmillan. London. '19.

Keynes, J. M. General theory of employment, interest, and money. Harcourt. New York. '65 [originally published in 1936].

Keynes, J. M. Treatise on money. Harcourt. New York. '30.

Lekachman, Robert. Age of Keynes. Random House. New York. '66.
    *Review:* Commentary. 42:91-2+. N. '66. Andrew Shonfield.

Musgrave, R. A. Theory of public finance; a study in public economy. McGraw-Hill. New York. '59.

National Bureau of Economic Research, Inc. Economic research and the Keynesian thinking of our times, by A. F. Burns. The Bureau. 261 Madison Ave. New York 10016. '46.
    26th annual report.

Paul, R. E. Taxation in the United States. Little. Boston. '54.

Rolph, E. R. and Break, G. F. Public finance. Ronald. New York. '61.

*Rostow, W. W. Stages of economic growth. Cambridge University Press. New York. '60.

Samuelson, P. A. Economics; an introductory analysis. 7th ed. McGraw-Hill. New York. '67.

*Seligman, E. R. A. Essays in taxation. Macmillan. New York. '25.

Shonfield, Andrew. Modern capitalism. Oxford University Press. New York. '65.

*Sprinkel, B. W. Destabilizing policies in a stable economy; testimony presented before the Joint Economic Committee of the Congress of the United States, February 17, 1967. Harris Trust and Savings Bank. Financial and Economic Research Department. P.O. Box 755. Chicago 60690.
    *Same.* United States. Congress. Joint Economic Committee. 1967 economic report of the President; hearings, February 15, 16, and 17, 1967; part 3. 90th Congress, 1st session. Supt. of Docs. Washington, D.C. 20402. '67. p 660-7.

*Stern, P. M. Great treasury raid. Random House. New York. '64.
    *Reprinted in this book:* Slow, quiet murder of tax reform [adaptation]. Harper's Magazine. 227:63-8. D. '63.
    *Reply with rejoinder:* 228:8+. Ap. '64.

Veritas Foundation, New York. Keynes at Harvard; economic deception as a political credo; Zygmund Dobbs, research director. rev. ed. The Foundation. 150 E. 35th St. New York 10016. '62 [originally published in 1961].

Wallace, H. A. Sixty million jobs. Simon and Schuster. New York. '45.

Wilkins, B. H. and Friday, C. B. eds. Economists of the New Frontier; an anthology. Random House. New York. '63.

PERIODICALS

America. 106:711, 744. Mr. 3-10, '62. Economic planning.

America. 115:314. S. 24, '66. Finally, fiscal policy to the rescue.

America. 116:803. Je. 3, '67. Raise taxes or cut spending.

Annals of the American Academy of Political and Social Science. 326:1-138. N. '59. Inflation; symposium, ed. by A. G. Buehler.

Annals of the American Academy of Political and Social Science. 359:71-80. My. '65. Allocation of responsibilities and resources among the three levels of government. J. C. Charlesworth.

Atlantic. 203:16+. Mr. '59. Private vs. public spending.

Atlantic. 204:12+. N. '59. Atlantic report.

Atlantic. 213:6+. Je. '64. Atlantic report; more flexible tax policy.

Bulletin of the Atomic Scientists. 16:97-102. Mr. '60. Goals, plans, and priorities in Soviet-American competition. D. J. Hekhuis.

Business Week. p 28-30. O. 17, '59. Booming free world sets pace for U.S.

Business Week. p. 92+, 132. My. 5, '62. Why the tax bill scares businessmen; with editorial comment.

*Business Week. p 128-30. Je. 23, '62. Income tax and how it grew.

Business Week. p 52-4+, 116. Ag. 25, '62. How taxes compare; here and in Europe; with editorial comment.

Business Week. p 150+. Je. 20, '64. Should we tax incomes less? tax sales or manufacturing more; with editorial comment.

Business Week. p 66+. Mr. 6, '65. Big issues: debt and taxes; report on study by forty-eight economists; with editorial comment.

Business Week. p 85-6+. S. 11, '65. Curbing the states' tax reach; taxes on out-of-state companies and on interstate sales.

*Business Week. p 70-3. Ja. 1, '66. Slippery path of prosperity; how to combine growth with full employment and stable prices.

Business Week. p 27. Ag. 6, '66. Guidelines sag under new siege; President Johnson's wage-price policy is reeling.

Business Week. p 168 F. 18, '67. Fed uses new tools to sharpen policy.

Business Week. p 35. Ap. 22, '67. Where the tax bill bogged down.

Business Week. p 96-8. My. 13, '67. New economics gets its lumps.

Business Week. p 200. My. 13, '67. Why fiscal policy must be flexible.

Catholic World. 201:108-12. My. '65. Religious tax exemptions and the First Amendment. J. J. Regan.

Changing Times. 19:31-2. N. '65. What computers are doing to your tax return.

Christian Science Monitor Magazine. p 2+. My. 4, '46. Uncle Sam and your job; Employment act of 1946 indicates swing toward government responsibility. J. S. Taylor.

Commonweal. 45:59. N. 1, '46. Country's new economic policy.

*Commonweal. 85:254-6. D. 2, '66. Economics and freedom. E. T. Chase.

Commonweal. 86:280-1. My. 26, '67. Our Rube Goldberg tax system; exorcising the deficit demon. H. S. Reuss.

Congressional Digest. 40:83-7. Mr. '61. Special economic message, February 2, 1961; excerpt. J. F. Kennedy.
  *Same:* Monthly Labor Review. 84:270-2. Mr. '61; Current History. 40:298-304. My. '61.

Dun's Review. 85:36-7+. F. '65. What's wrong with our tax system? interview; ed. by G. R. Rosen. M. M. Caplin.

Dun's Review. 88:41-2+. O. '66. Flaw in the new economics. W. F. Butler.

Dun's Review. 89:5. Ja. '67. Through a glass, brightly.

*Editorial Research Reports. 1, no11:203-19. Mr. 24, '65. Excise tax cuts and the economy. R. L. Worsnop.

*Editorial Research Reports. 2, no 21:887-904. D. 2, '66. Maintenance of prosperity. R. L. Worsnop.

Foreign Policy Bulletin. 39:54-6. D. 15, '59. Communist timetable for 1960, what odds? V. M. Dean.

*Fortune. 32:158-9+. O. '45. Toward full employment. Milton Gilbert.

Fortune. 32:160-1+. O. '45. More job givers wanted. S. H. Slichter.

Fortune. 60:62+. Ag. '59. Shoji screen.

Fortune. 66:88-91+. O. '62. Priority of politics over economics. John Davenport.

Fortune. 67:72-5+. Ja. '63. Real case for a tax cut. Max Ways.

Fortune. 67:79-80. Mr. '63. How to save the tax cut.

Fortune. 67:91-2. Je. '63. How good is the Kennedy style?

Fortune. 70:104-7+. D. '64. Next turn in taxes. E. K. Faltermayer.

Fortune. 74:29. S. '66. Classic climax.

Fortune. 74:31-2. O. '66. President's package.

Fortune. 74:113-14. O. '66. Case for doing almost nothing.

Fortune. 74:152-5+. D. '66. There wasn't any panic at 23 Wall. John McDonald.

Fortune. 75:101-2. F. '67. Tax with a question mark.

Fortune. 75:110-15+. Mr. '67. U.S. economy enters a new era. William Bowen.

Harvard Business Review. 40:81-91. Ja. '62. Economics, politics, and the Fed. G. L. Bach.

Life. 54:4. Ja. 11, '63. Why we are urging cuts in taxes now.

Life. 54:4. Mr. 1, '63. How to rescue the tax cut.

Life: 61:4. Ag. 19, '66. L.B.J. and his splintered guideposts.

Nation. 160:664-5. Je. 16, '45. Fight for S. 380, the Full employment bill.

Nation. 188:201-4. Mr. 7, '59. Dilemma of inflation. P. M. Sweezy.

Nation. 194:260-2. Mr. 24, '62. Paradoxes of taxation. P. L. Bernstein.

Nation. 195:462. D. 29, '62. Behind the tax cuts.

Nation. 200:643-5. Je. 14, '65. Tax-cut habit. R. A. Musgrave.

National Review. 13:421+. D. 4, '62. What is sound taxation?

National Review. 18:1032. O. 18, '66. Crash of '66.

Nation's Business. 50:40-1+. N. '62. Why we must cut taxes now. W. W. Heller.

Nation's Business. 55:36-9+. Ja '67. What's happening to the boom.

Nation's Business. 55:82-4. F. '67. Way out of the tax thicket? L. E. Kust.

Nation's Business. 55:42-4+. Ap. '67. How to keep the bloom on the boom; forecast from top executives.

New Republic. 143:15-18. Jl. 25, '60. Growth through taxation. James Tobin.
> Reply: 143:17-19. O. 10, '60. L. H. Keyserling.

New Republic. 143:10. D. 5, '60. Prosperity unlimited.

New Republic. 146:9. F. 12, '62. Flexible tax rates.

New Republic. 147:3-4. Ag. 13, '62. Economics 1-A.

*New Republic. 147:15-19. Ag. 13, '62. A tax cut now? Emile Benoit.

New Republic. 147:14-15. Ag. 27, '62. Deficits and economic growth. M. J. Kust.
> Reply: 147:17. S. 17, '62. A. H. Hansen.

New Republic. 147:9-35+. O. 20, '62. Time for a Keynes; an inquiry into what new economic thinking is required for the US in the sixties; symposium.
> Reply entitled More than Keynes. 147:19-20. D. 1, '62. Benjamin Caplan and Harald Malmgren.

New Republic. 148:22. Mr. 22, '63. Andrew Mellon on tax cuts. D. F. Swanson.

New Republic. 150:3-4. F. 15, '64. After the tax cut.

New Republic. 152:6. My. 29, '65. Tax reform gets lost.

New Republic. 155:9-14. S. 3, '66. Check the boom? James Tobin.

New Republic. 155:4. O. '22, '66. T.R.B. from Washington; economic turnabout.
> Discussion: 155:38. N. 12, 44-5. N. 26, '66.

New Republic. 156:17-19. Mr. 4, '67. National economic policy for '67; excerpts from addresses before Joint Economic Committee of Congress, February 16. J. Tobin; A. H. Hansen.

*New York Times. p 26. My. 18, '65. Text of President Johnson's message to Congress calling for reductions in excise taxes, May 17, 1965.

*New York Times. p E6. F. 20, '66. The other big question is: will the economy overheat? E. L. Dale, Jr.

*New York Times. p 76. S. 11, '66. President's tax proposal: a product of fear and study. Max Frankel.

*New York Times. p 44. My. 18, '67. Fight for flexibility in tax structure appears to be lost. M. J. Rossant.

New York Times. p 1+. N. 20, '67. 6 in Common Market move to back a loan to Britain. Henry Tanner.

New York Times. p 1+. N. 20, '67. Wilson implores Britons to help aid the economy. Anthony Lewis.

New York Times. p 1+. N. 22, '67. Pound is strong. J. M. Lee.

New York Times. p 1+. N. 24, '67. Gold-buying wave swells, battering dollar in Europe.

New York Times. p F 1+. N. 26, '67. British trade surplus still elusive. Gerd Wilcke.

New York Times. p F 1+. N. 26, '67. Devaluation only a start for London. R. E. Mooney.

New York Times. p F 1. N. 26, '67. Doubt raised on system of liquidity. H. E. Heinemann.

*New York Times Book Review. p 1+. My. 16, '65. Came the revolution [review of 1965 edition of General theory of employment, interest, and money, by J. M. Keynes]. J. K. Galbraith.

New York Times Magazine. p 7+. F. 8, '59. Now the challenge of an economic Sputnik. Barbara Ward.

New York Times Magazine. p 23+. Mr. 8, '59. Arguments for creeping inflation. S. H. Slichter.

New York Times Magazine. p 9+. N. 1, '59. Marx was wrong and so is Khrushchev. A. A. Berle, Jr.

New York Times Magazine. p 27+. Mr. 18, '62. We must grow, or we sink. A. H. Hansen.

*New York Times Magazine. p 55. Ag. 5, '62. 100 years of income outgo. R. B. Morris.

New York Times Magazine. p 26+. Ap. 14, '63. Gap between economist and politician. S. E. Harris.

*New York Times Magazine. p 22+. O. 27, '63. The West debates the great growth issue. Barbara Ward.

New York Times Magazine. p 33+. D. 1, '63. Machines are more important than people (yes or no?); attitude test. P. M. Stern.

New York Times Magazine. p32+. Mr. 21, '65. Tax reform, four basic ideas. M. D. Reagan.

*New York Times Magazine. p 36-7+. Ap. 4, '65. We are depression (but not recession) proof. E. L. Dale, Jr.

*New York Times Magazine. p 50-1+. S. 18, '66. What went wrong? Another look at the new economics. E. L. Dale, Jr.

New York Times Magazine. p 38-9+. N. 5, '67. Three reasons for prosperity. E. L. Dale, Jr.

New Yorker. 38:21. Ja. 12, '63. Notes and comments.

Newsweek. 53:100. Je. 1, '59. Great delusion. Raymond Moley.

Newsweek. 57:81. F. 20, '61. Kennedian economics. Henry Hazlitt.

Newsweek. 59:32. Je. 18, '62. Neither Smith nor Keynes. Kenneth Crawford.

Newsweek. 59:17-20. Je. 25, '62. Myths and men and the economy [with excerpts from President Kennedy's Yale commencement address and comments by businessmen].

Newsweek. 60:30. Ag. 27, '62. Politics and taxes. Kenneth Crawford.

Newsweek. 61:77. Ja. 28, '63. Invitation to inflation. Henry Hazlitt.

Newsweek. 61:23-4. Mr. 11, '63. How to cut taxes? cut the reforms.

Newsweek. 65:66. My. 31, '65. Keynes revolution.

Newsweek. 65:82. Je. 21, '65. New orthodoxy. Henry Hazlitt.

Newsweek. 68:63. Ag. 1, '66. Keep the lid on, fellows.

Newsweek. 68:79. Ag. 22, '66. Guidelines for the guidelines. L. B. Johnson.

Newsweek. 68:82+. S. 19, '66. Inflation: the White House acts; five-point package.

Newsweek. 68:79. O. 3, '66. LBJ's economic baling wire; anti-inflation moves.

Newsweek. 68:46. O. 31, '66. Woe is us. Kenneth Crawford.

Newsweek. 69:77. Mr. 13, '67. Fed tunes up a drifting economy.

Newsweek. 69:94. Mr. 20, '67. Non-tax increase. H. C. Wallich.

Newsweek. 69:80. My. 1, '67. Keeping the score. P. A. Samuelson.

Newsweek. 69:85. My. 29, '67. Finetuning; fiscal and monetary motions destabilize the economy. H. C. Wallich.

Reader's Digest. 78:45-9. Ap. '61. Let's get off the tax road to ruin. J. S. Seidman.

Reader's Digest. 81:81-4. S. '62. We can't spend ourselves rich. H. F. Byrd.

Reporter. 26:19-22. Je. 21, '62. Mr. Kennedy's guidelines; are they drawn too tight? A. H. Raskin.

Reporter. 28:22-5. F. 14, '63. Economic education of John F. Kennedy. M. J. Rossant.
    *Discussion.* 28:10+. Mr. 14, '63.

Reporter. 28:20-3. Je. 6, '63. Case for tax reform. J. A. Pechman.

Saturday Evening Post. 233:36+. N. 5, '60. America must grow. Walter Lippmann and F. M. Bator.

Saturday Evening Post. 236:15-19, 82. My. 18, '63. Spending into trouble; with editorial comment. D. D. Eisenhower.
    *Abridged version entitled* We are spending ourselves into trouble. Reader's Digest. 83:60-8. Jl. '63.

Saturday Evening Post. 236:17. D. 21, '63. More on the great tax myth. Stewart Alsop.

Saturday Evening Post. 237:92. D. 5, '64. Let's cut taxes again.

Saturday Review. 47:30-2. Ja. 11, '64. What the tax cut can do. F. B. Wilde.

Science. 128:1258-62. N. 21, '58. Mr. Keynes and the Day of Judgment. D. M. Wright.
    *Reply with rejoinder.* 129:1164-6. Ap. 24, '59. P. A. Klein.

Science. 133:367-9. F. 10, '61. Kennedy's economics; the dismal science made cheery.

Science. 133:742-4. Mr. 17, '61. Educating the public: to win broad support for his program Kennedy assumes the role of mass educator.

Senior Scholastic. 76:8-11+. Ap. 13, '60. Japan, a new sun rises.

Senior Scholastic. 82:5-7. Ja. 30. '63. Taxes; to cut or not to cut . . . that is the question.

Senior Scholastic. 82:10-11. Mr. 27, '63. Tax cut before tax reform? a pro and con discussion.

Senior Scholastic. 86:12-15. Ap. 1, '65. State taxes: problem of soaring demands, shrinking sources.

Senior Scholastic. 87:12-16. Ja. 14, '66. Rise of the new economics.

Senior Scholastic. 88:6-7. Ap. 1, '66. Government and the economy; planning for prosperity.

Senior Scholastic. 89:6-9. O. '14, '66. Monetary policy+fiscal policy+politics=?

Senior Scholastic. 89:11-13. D. 9, '66. Government and the economy; tricky business of managing prosperity.

*Time. 73:90. F. 16, '59. Is the nation growing fast enough?
          *Same abridged:* Reader's Digest. 74:263-4. My. '59.

Time. 73:22-3. Mr. 16, '59. Battle behind the budget battle, is red ink a tonic or a poison?

Time. 79:17-19. Je. 22, '62. Myths & taxes.

Time. 80:8. Ag. 24, '62. Politics versus policy; question of tax cut.

Time. 81:19-22. Ja. 11, '63. Idea on the march; House Ways and Means Committee.

*Time. 86:64-67B. D. 31, '65. We are all Keynesians now.

Time. 88:65. Ag. 26, '66. Bankers' brakes.

Time. 88:87. S. 23, '66. Day of the little bulls; Johnson's anti-inflation package.

Time. 88:103. S. 30, '66. With baling wire; latest anti-inflation moves.

Time. 88:47-50+. D. 30, '66. Year of tight money and where it will lead.

Time. 89:81. Mr. 24, '67. Billion-dollar decision.

Time. 90:29-32. N. 24, '67. Britain: the agony of the pound.

U.S. News & World Report. 46:80-3. Ap. 20, '59. Japan's miracle.

U.S. News & World Report. 50:113-14. My. 1, '61. Flexible taxes: latest idea in Britain.

U.S. News & World Report. 52:120. Mr. 19, '62. Preventing recessions? David Lawrence.

U.S. News & World Report. 52:103-5. Ap. 2, '62. What's wrong with tax bill; as business, Congress see it.

U.S. News & World Report. 52:120-2. Ap. 23, '62. Planning by taxes, how Britain and Canada do it.

U.S. News & World Report. 53:53-6. S. 10, '62. ABC's of any cut in taxes.

U.S. News & World Report. 53:44-5. D. 10, '62. What a 10-billion-dollar tax cut would mean.

U.S. News & World Report. 54:43-53. F. 4, '63. Dangers of tax cut as seen by Congress; with summary of message to Congress by John F. Kennedy.

U.S. News & World Report. 54:38-9. Mr. 4, '63. Thrift vs. borrowing, which way good times?

U.S. News & World Report. 58:82-4. Mr. 8, '65. What other countries are doing about taxes.

U.S. News & World Report. 59:85. Jl. 26, '65. Tax theory that has proved out in practice.

*U.S. News & World Report. 61:29-31. S. 19, '66. Is a money crisis near?

U.S. News & World Report. 61:112. D. 5, '66. To spend more, to tax more, or to economize? David Lawrence.

U.S. News & World Report. 61:27-9. D. 12, '66. Chances now for a tax increase; with excerpt from address by A. F. Burns.

U.S. News & World Report. 62:32-3. F. 6, '67. Business prospects in 1967, as LBJ looks ahead.

U.S. News & World Report. 62:60-3. F. 27, '67. Your taxes: out of hand? [views of top economists].

U.S. News & World Report. 62:63. F. 27, '67. Taxes in major nations; how the burden in U.S. compares.

U.S. News & World Report. 62:72. Mr. 13, '67. Dilemma for Johnson: who is to manage the dollar.

U.S. News & World Report. 62:118+. Mr. 20, '67. If U.S. shares taxes with states; where money will go [with chart].

U.S. News & World Report. 62:109. My. 1, '67. What's happened to a simple tax plan?

U.S. News & World Report. 62:111. My. 1, '67. Tough talk on U.S. tax policies.

Vital Speeches of the Day. 25:433-6. My. 1, '59. Some observations of fiscal conservatism. J. P. Warburg.

Vital Speeches of the Day. 27:648-55. Ag. 15, '61. American tax system: national, state, local; address, June 12, 1961. R. A. Freeman.

Vital Speeches of the Day. 28:610-14. Ag. 1, '62. Developing dialogue on economic growth; address June 18, 1962. R. J. Saulnier.

Vital Speeches of the Day. 29:226-30. F. 1, '63. State of the Union; address, January 14, 1963. J. F. Kennedy.
    *Same:* Current History. 44:174-6+. Mr. '63; *Excerpts:* Department of State Bulletin. 48:159-64. F. 4, '63; *Summary:* Senior Scholastic. 82:15-17. Ja. 30, '63.

Vital Speeches of the Day. 33:24-8. O. 15, '66. Fiscal and monetary policy; address, September 12, 1966. L. H. Olsen.

Vital Speeches of the Day. 33:278-82. F. 15, '67. Political economics. P. A. Rinfret.

Wall Street Journal. p 10. Ja. 23, '64. Business cycle is here to stay; editorial.

Wall Street Journal. p 1+. F. 21, '64. Spending step-up; most persons, firms plan to put tax-cut funds into new outlays.

*Wall Street Journal. p 3+. F. 27, '64. Waiting for the boom. R. F. Janssen.

Wall Street Journal. p 1+. F. 1, '65. Tax-cut impact; firms say excise drop would spark economy, bring other benefits.

Wall Street Journal. p 18. My. 19, '65. LBJ's arguments for excise tax cut; editorial.

Wall Street Journal. p 10. Je. 4, '65. Tax policy of Federal Government.

Wall Street Journal. p 1+. Je. 18, '65. Excise tax reduction likely to bring blend of confusion and joy. A. J. Large.

Wall Street Journal. p 1. Ag. 17, '65. Surprise surpluses; state tax collections soar above estimates, easing fiscal squeeze.

Wall Street Journal. p 1+. O. 5, '65. Trimming taxes; Administration studies further cuts in levies for individuals, firms. R. F. Janssen.

Wall Street Journal. p 16. D. 16, '65. Federal officials gird for tax boost though White House says no.

Wall Street Journal. p 3. Ap. 1, '66. LBJ asks spending restraint to avoid tax boost.

Wall Street Journal. p 3. My. 5, '66. W. M. Martin sees tax boost needed to fight inflation.

*Wall Street Journal. p 1. My. 17, '66. Debate over taxes.

Wall Street Journal. p 2. My. 27, '66. David Rockefeller asks for tax boost.

Wall Street Journal. p 17. Je. 14, '66. U.S. should have standby mechanism for quick tax rate action Bank for International Settlements proposes in annual report.

Wall Street Journal. p 18. Je. 21, '66. Taxation alone can't cope with inflation; editorial.

Wall Street Journal. p 1. Jl. 7, '66. Tax outlook; White House mulls rise in 1967 levies.

Wall Street Journal. p 12. N. 25, '66. Is taxation or reduced Federal spending best way to end inflation; editorial.

Wall Street Journal. p 4. N. 28, '66. Heller urges balance between monetary & fiscal policy.

Wall Street Journal. p 12. Ap. 21, '67. Tax credit bill stalls as Democrats feud in Senate over campaign fund law repeal.

*Wall Street Journal. p 2. Je. 16, '67. More political control over Reserve Board is urged by Saxon, citing its planning role.

Wall Street Journal. p 1+. N. 20, '67. After devaluation. Ray Vicker.

Wall Street Journal. p 1+. N. 21, '67. British goods' prices may not fall as fast or far as expected. Lee Berton.

Wall Street Journal. p 1+. N. 22, '67. Devaluation ripples. Ray Vicker.

Wall Street Journal. p 1+. N. 28, '67. Dollar's foe. Ray Vicker.

Yale Review. 52:188-204. D. '62. Emperor's old clothes; the folklore of capitalism revisited. T. W. Arnold.